DAVID BOWIE, UFOS, WITCHCRAFT, COCAINE AND PARANOIA

The Occult Saga of Walli Elmlark
The "Rock N' Roll" Witch of New York

By Timothy Green Beckley

Photos by Helen Hovey

Art by Carol Ann Rodriguez

Graphics and Layout by Tim R. Swartz

Includes Original Spells and Wiccan Lore

INNER LIGHT/GLOBAL COMMUNICATIONS

P.O. Box 753
New Brunswick, NJ 08903

mrufo8@hotmail.com

DAVID BOWIE, UFOS, WITCHCRAFT, COCAINE AND PARANOIA

The Occult Saga of Walli Elmlark
The "Rock N' Roll" Witch of New York
By Timothy Green Beckley

Published in the United States of America by Inner Light/Global Communications, PO Box 753 - New Brunswick, NJ 08903

Staff Members:
Timothy G. Beckley, Publisher
Carol Ann Rodriguez, Assistant to the Publisher
Sean Casteel, General Associate Editor
Tim R. Swartz, Graphics and Formatting
William Kern, Editorial and Art Consultant

www.ConspiracyJournal.com
Order Hot Line: 1-732-602-3407
PayPal: MrUFO8@hotmail.com

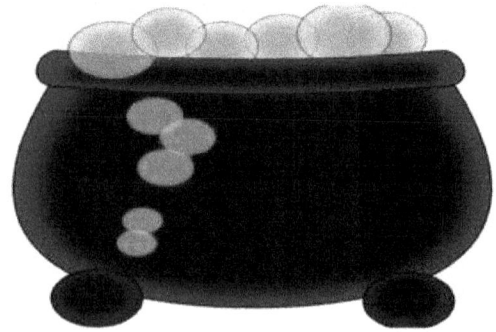

CONTENTS

Walli Elmlark © The Helen Hovey Collection.

HOMAGE TO THE SUN AND MOON GODS OF THE WICCAN FAITH
ART ©CAROL ANN RODRIGUEZ.

Walli Elmlark © The Helen Hovey Collection.

BLESSED BE

I am going to tell you a story.

This book has so many intriguing elements and surprises that I can definitely say that there is something for every taste within these lovingly written pages.

Walli Elmlark

It is a book about the occult. About witchcraft (the religion of WICCA in particular). It's a study guide on how to perform magick and cast spells. And about rock and roll and some very famous musicians, and other counter culture artists who it could be said had some very unusual habits.

Some may say this "*book of shadows*" is loaded with gossip and they certainly would not be wrong. Is it overly sensationalistic? That's for you to decide. But above all else it is about one person in particular...**WALLI ELMLARK!** A unique lady whose career and life was multifaceted. She was known for casting spells and that she did on - and for - some very celebrated individuals - among them David Bowie who admittedly owed his life to the White Witch of New York.

And while Walli has passed from this realm, grievingly at her own hands, decades later she is still fondly remembered by those she mesmerized in one way or another.

So light your candles - play some rock music as loud as you can and come along with us on our mad adventure back in time to the Sixties and Seventies. I guarantee it will be a crazy ass trip you won't soon forget.

Tim Beckley

New York City 2019

mrufo8@hotmail.com

Timothy Green Beckley

Photo by April Troiani

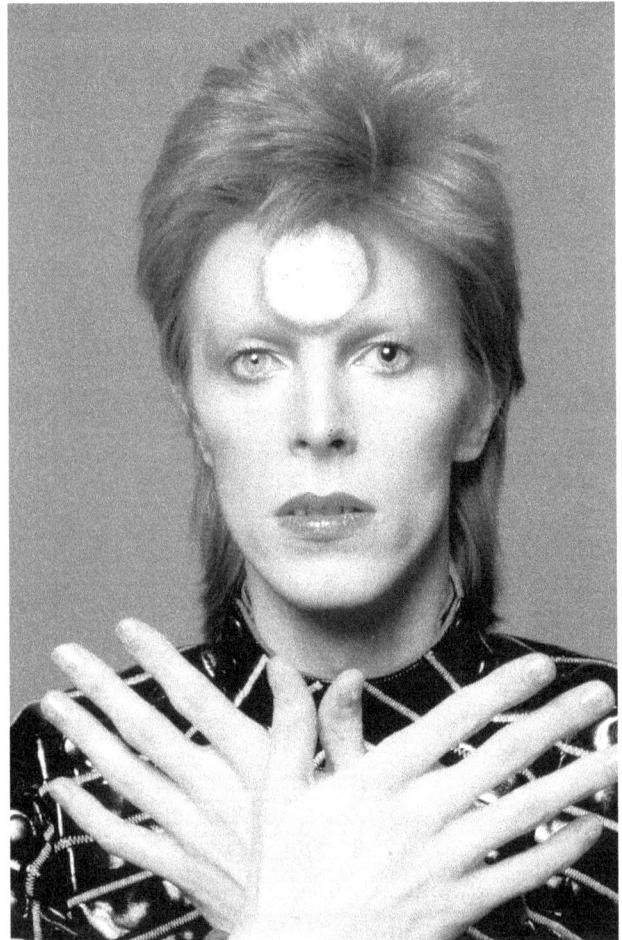

Ziggy Stardust

1.
MUST BE THE SEASON OF THE WITCH

IN the beginning there was rock and roll!

All the learned mystics tell us that life is meant to be a learning experience. It doesn't matter what your job or position in this world. Be it construction worker, teacher, scientist, doctor - or, yes, even rock star.

The 3 "Amigos" of Rock 'N' Roll and witchcraft --
Walli Elmlark, Helen Hovey and Tim Beckley (circa early 1970's
photographer unknown).

The Fillmore East had recently closed (June 27, 1971) and for a while there was a vacuum as far as decent live rock and roll music goes in New York City. Promoter Bill Graham had actually started to bad mouth the up and coming acts indicating they lacked talent and rambled on about the sophistication of the audience.

Maybe he was a bit sour that he hadn't been the organizer of Woodstock, as he didn't seem to vibe with the concept of rock festivals and booking artists into large venues. Said Graham: "I continue to deplore the exploitation of the gigantic-hall concerts, many of them with high-priced tickets. The sole incentive of too many has simply become money. The conditions for such performances, besides lacking intimacy, are professionally impossible according to my standards."

Now considered "classic rockers" some of the best musicians of the era hit the stage at the Academy of Music.

BITTER! BITTER! BITTER!

As far as rock and roll goes I had been an "early bloomer." My first album was by the flamboyant Little Richard and I played Chuck Berry's "*Sweet Little Sixteen*" over and over again (actually, I was more into the B side which was "*Johnny Be Good*," circa 1958). When I was old enough to get on a bus by myself, I would make the brief trek from Jersey to Manhattan and started going to some of the clubs in Greenwich Village. Drinking age was 18 and there was no such thing as "proper ID" in those days. Some of the popular live music venues were Gerde's Folk City, Cafe Au Go Go, and Cafe Wha?

I keep no secret of the fact that I hated folk music. I was positively not a fan of Bob Dylan and Peter, Paul and Mary's "Puff The Magic Dragon" didn't light my fire. But I did groove on a more high energy musical scene that was being played out in the Village's more hip establishments. I made it my business to catch some really powerful artists in the early days of establishing their careers – one musician in particular got my attention and totally blew me away – it was a young flashy guitarist named Jimi Hendrix!

For a two drink minimum you could stay for both sets at any of the dark bohemian clubs that dotted Bleeker and Mcdougal streets. And that's where Jimi and others were cutting their teeth into the wee hours of the morning (closing time 4 AM, after hour's clubs always open for those "with the proper connections").

One evening I was out and about just wandering the streets of the lower East Side perhaps with a flask of brandy in my coat pocket when "by chance" I happened to stumble at the corner of 6th Street and Second Avenue. The side door to the Fillmore East was open as that's where the band's roadies hauled in their equipment, but you could hear the loud, pulsating rock music flowing from inside just like you were hanging out backstage (which technically you would have been if you stepped twenty feet beyond the stage door security barrier).

A former opera house, then a vaudeville theater, the once opulant Academy became the belly wick for rock music after the closing of the Fillmore East.

As I started to go on my way, I noticed that security was being provided by a member of a well known motorcycle club whose job it was to make sure no one snuck into the auditorium or no one left with equipment that wasn't rightfully theirs. I guess we nodded a "hello" to each other and started to shoot the shit about rock and roll.

Most hard core bikers would normally keep the conversation to a minimum and indicate that you should be on your way. But after a brief conversation "Fat Joe" asked me if I wanted to go in so I passed through the back door of the Fillmore to watch Black Sabbath for the rest of the night and thus to become a regular fixture on the back stage New York City rock scene. I always tell people I went out that night and never came home. Truth is I am not home yet!

After the Fillmore closed (I did book a few acts in there after the theater was renamed. Turns out the new promoters hadn't a clue and ended up stiffing some of the bands I heard), we of the rock and roll high life (take that anyway you want) were looking for a new place to call home. I had become managing editor of a weekly "rival" to the hip *"Village Voice."* The "*Manhattan Gazette*," a rather tacky unattractive tabloid, was left in the lobbies of apartment buildings throughout the city (I know because in addition to my editorial talents, it was my job to dump the papers anywhere there was a doorman who allowed us to leave a stack, probably throwing them out the moment my back was turned).

The publisher, a middle aged woman with little foresight or charisma, was not a fan of rock music. In fact, I'm not sure what she liked, but I had my own office in a very impressive building just off Central Park, and I somehow convinced her to let me do a music column.

The action had, as it turned out, moved just a few blocks uptown to the once elegant Astor Opera House which opened on Fourteenth Street and Irving Plaza in 1854. Later, in the 1920s, it became the Academy of Music, a vaudeville theater – say hello to the spirits of George and Gracie if your every in the neighborhood.

A trade paper reports on promoter Howard Stein's career.

By the time it reinvented itself as a rock "palace," the three tiered, 3600 seat, auditorium had become a bit thread bare, but it certainly was still piss elegant compared to the Fillmore East.

Stepping forward to fit the bill as a much needed rock impresario was Howard Stein who not only took over where Bill Graham left off, but far surpassed him, certainly in elegance, eventually promoting such super stars as David Bowie, The Who, and the Rolling Stones. The son of loan shark Ruby Stein who was murdered by the Westies and dumped headless into Jamaica Bay, Howard knew how to spot a contender who was due by destiny to explode upon the scene to become a rock icon. His motto was, "Never listen to what the critics have to say. Watch the reaction of the audience." And that he did as he pretty much filled the house every Friday and Saturday night, with an 8 and an 11 pm show. Many a night I left the Academy with the sun coming up (always be sure to carry shades if you're planning to stay out late in the City).

Lila and Helen. Ms Schulman introduced us to Walli.

ENTER WALLI THE WITCH, AND HELEN THE PHOTOGRAPHER

At the same time I was rocking the casaba I had founded one of the first, if not the very first, metaphysical centers in the country. The New York School of Occult Arts and Sciences was located in a 2200 square foot loft on the second floor of an apartment building on 14th Street between Seventh and Eighth Avenues. It was just "down the road" from the Academy, about six blocks away as guitar picks fly. We had lectures and workshops on

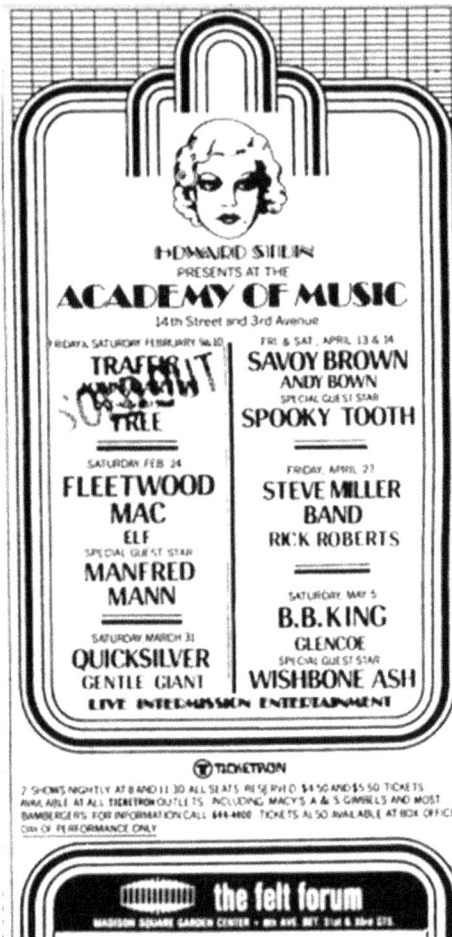

A typical ad that ran in the Village Voice announcing forthcoming shows. Logo was created by Lila Schulman.

UFOs, Tarot Cards, Witchcraft, Prophecy, Astral Projection, as well as lessons in how to use the Ouija Board (safely!) and held midnight séances every Saturday with the medium Kitty Steele, a former model from Michigan.

To some degree the rock music was a sort of release from my organizational and promotional duties at the occult school. I was, indeed, a promoter in my own right and the witch I am about to introduce was our main headliner.

There were quite a few celebrities interested in the occult, and they showed up from time to time, like Doctor John the Night Tripper who came in full voodoo regalia to be photographed by Helen Hovey, who was honing her skills as a shutterbug. Having met in our late teens, Helen and I had become fast friends. We attended many of the same concerts together at the Academy, she working out of the orchestra pit and me standing up against the wall near the back stage door where the music was as loud as can be, but you were positioned only a couple of feet away from being on the stage! Hey, a couple of times I was!

Our successful posturing at the Academy had come about thanks to Howard Stein's assistant. Wishing to be on the guest list as part of our journalistic duties, we had called Stein's office and were put in touch with Lila Schulman who sat at the front desk answering the phone, typing up contracts and organizing the guest list. Lila was an art graduate and had designed the logo used in all the Academy of Music ads announcing forthcoming shows.

Somehow the conversation got around to the occult and I remember helping Lila find a ring that she had lost somewhere in her apartment through "remote viewing." It had fallen behind a bureau if I recall, and that is where I had psychically visualized it. She was most impressed having dug it out from behind the rather heavy chest of drawers, pretty much where I said she would find it.

SUPERMAN HERE!

So positively affected—I say half in jest—by my extrasensory skills, Lila wrote me a letter, in which she said she wanted Helen and I to meet a particular female rock columnist who was making herself known back stage by giving spiritual advice to some of the more open minded musicians who did not poo poo super-normal matters that we were all so fascinated with during this time period.

Walli Elmlark had been raised in a Jewish family but had found the tenants of witchcraft more to her liking. She had become a member of the Wiccan faith, a form of paganism, going far back into antiquity and pre-dating Christianity by God knows how long. Walli was quick to point out that she was NOT a Satanist, nor did she wish harm onto others, but was a good witch, or "white witch, casting beneficial spells and using candles and gemstones for "self empowerment." But more on Walli's beliefs and philosophy as we proceed.

In folklore, witches are often portrayed in negative ways, being malicious or sinister by nature. Many are depicted as archetypal "old crones," well past their prime, who are frequently scary and "rough around the edges" appearance wise. These are the witches that Hansel and Gretel run shitless away from trying to get back out of the woods.

Helen Hovey recalls meeting Walli for the first time. "She stood out in the crowd, even among the long haired hipsters and mod, English-style, dressers. She was a very imposing individual, with a very striking figure.

"Dressed in black with dark make up and silver jewelry and a green streak in her hair, Walli's fashion sense was trailblazing, not really goth but certainly cutting edge. You knew she was someone special, not just the average journalist with pen in paper out to get a good quote."

Helen points out that Walli was already famous in England writing for "Melody Maker" which was a more musical than political publication like "*Rolling Stone*," but in the same hip, avant-garde, vain. She was also a columnist for "Circus," a flashy glossy newsstand publication which was more fan orientated, aimed at a teen audience who were prone to put up posters of their rave faves on their bedroom walls.

Right off the bat, Helen knew that the "White Witch of New York," which had become Walli's endearing moniker, would make a great subject for a photo shoot.

"I remember she was rather shy at first when I asked if she would pose for me. But by the time I had arranged the lighting and selected my lenses for the shoot she seemed to be at ease. It almost seemed after a while that we had known each other for a life time. She was by no means a diva though she could have been with all her famous friends."

Turns out, Helen found Walli to be very down to earth and they became fast friends.

"I remember she had luminescent stars on her ceiling which glowed in the dark. I most definitely have fond memories of being with her. She was wise beyond her years and seemed to have a window into the future of rock and roll. She certainly had a keen ear for an up and coming performer. I remember she had a lot of rock and roll people coming in and out of her apartment. Besides being interviewed, they were all anxious to hear what she had to say as word of her witchcraft activities began to spread. Some even wanted her to do a psychic reading for them or offer them a specific colored good luck candle."

I would have to agree that Walli had charisma, though she was not flawless. I, myself, found her most captivating - let's lay it on the line and say damn right bewitching if we must. Hey witches can be sexy I was to find out, and she was one of those kind.

I find it somewhat amazing that decades have gone by since her passing, but that she is still remembered in high regard as a beneficial light in the lives of those who came in contact with both in and out of the music business.

Walli has long since passed from the earth plane, but not from the thoughts and memories of those she helped tutor along their spiritual paths when they often needed guidance the most.

Helen, soon landed a job with Howard, moving from the photographers pit to the VIP Green Room as hostess, greeting the guests and working with catering, making sure there were the contracted for bottles of liquor, and food requested by the performers and their managers as stated in their contract with the promoter.

Helen rapidly moved up the ranks working in promotion at several record labels in NY and LA, including Bell Records, Private Stock and Atlantic. When disco began to push out rock and roll (boo), Helen found herself going out at night to the clubs in order to acquaint the DJ's with the artists she represented, most fondly Frankie Valli.

But this book is about Walli and even to this day Helen remembers Walli most fondly and is happy to share some of the images that remain from that initial photo session as well as those of Marc Bolan, who Walli, as we shall see, considered very much a true Wizard, while David Bowie always remained the space man to her. I think you will agree that this is a fascinating tale of pop culture and its stars, the occult, witchcraft and the lives of people whom the White Witch of New York effected the most. It is truly a tale of enchantment - though it does have a tragic ending.

Helen went from photographer to Green Room hostess
at the Academy.

A UFO perches over David Bowie --
courtesy of and©by artist Nicholas May.
https://web.arhive.org/web/20161007195853/
http://nicholasmay.net/

2.

UFOS, WITCHCRAFT, THE ANTI-CHRIST AND DAVID BOWIE'S SECRET STASH

There's a starman waiting in the sky
He'd like to come and meet us
But he thinks he'd blow our minds
There's a starman waiting in the sky
He's told us not to blow it
'Cause he knows it's all worthwhile
He told me
Let the children lose it
Let the children use it
Let all the children boogie
Music and lyrics by David Bowie

HIS arrival was hugely hyped.

Everyone who was a member of the music media would do almost anything to be granted an interview.

They were interested to know what this "visitor from Mars" had in mind when traveling to this side of the Atlantic and if he planned to stay around for a while, as if he had just arrived from the Red Planet for real - and just maybe he had!

Walli Elmlark knew David Bowie. He had been to her apartment. They were striking up a friendship, getting some sort of bond going. True, she wrote a very prestigious column for *"Circus Magazine,"* but beyond the attention she could give the newly arrived pop singer from Britain whose career was just blossoming in the U.S., they seemed to have a lot in common on a personal level.

Bowie was really interested in the same things Walli was.

Witchcraft!

Magick!

UFOs!

And he wasn't just an idol curiosity seeker. No! He had experiences of his own. Had seen UFOs. Believed in time travel. Sought out other dimensions, all within a spiritual framework.

Walli introduced me to David and we shook hands. There was a line of reporters wanting their shot at speaking with him, so I didn't press on because of the press you might say. I did speak with him on the phone - he called looking for Walli, but hell who could blame him as she had a certain type of knowledge that he wanted to tap into. And he did reach out to me in recent years since her passing, wanting to know what lead to her disturbing death. Unfortunately, the details I had were fragmented!

I won't tell you what name he used as his email address, but you would get a kick out of it. He genuinely wanted to know what had become of the witch that had been a big part of his personal support system. Like most celebrities they drift off into other facets of their career and generally don't have the time nor inclination to look back to the days when they were just starting out, and to the people who once surrounded them. It's not being mean, it's just how the world turns.

Born David Jones, just outside of London in January 1947, this British lad later changed his name professionally to David Bowie, to eventually become one of the most influential figures in pop music history. His immense popularity and diversification of style cannot be disputed, Bowie was a musical genius. As a human being he was certainly not without his weaknesses. His quizzical mind and a little help from a friend – Walli Elmlark! – got him through troubled waters paving the way for the best years of his life.

IN THE DAYS OF ZIGGY STARDUST

I met David during his original tour of the United States when he had adopted the stage persona of "Ziggy Stardust," a sort of lost-in-space androgynous alien, complete with cosmic makeup and a painted lightning bolt zigzagging across his face down to his naked chest.

Ziggy Stardust started it all as Bowie went from spaceman to occultist.

Before venturing across the pond, Bowie had caused quite a sensation in the British press not only because of his outlandish - to some - image of a rock and roller from Mars, but also because of his independent and very liberal sexual lifestyle, a life style that had started to catch on in the Sixties and was still expanding here on the continent.

Bowie was introduced to me at the RCA studios in Manhattan by a most bedazzling young witch. In addition to "*Melody Maker*" in the UK, Walli had been given the opportunity to write a regular column for "*Circus Magazine*." "*Circus*" was a sort of heavy metal version of "*Rolling Stone*" that was printed on glossy paper with color photos of pop star favorites who were emerging on the then-burgeoning heavy metal and glam rock scenes.

Summing up – with apologies for perhaps being a bit repetitive - at the time I was wearing several hats. I was promoting a number of local rock bands who never quite "made it" big, editing the widely distributed "*UFO Review*" (the world's only official flying saucer newspaper), and running the New York School Of Occult Arts and Sciences, among the first metaphysical centers in the country where you could take classes in anything from astral projection to hypnosis to witchcraft. Which is how I came to be acquainted with Walli Elmlark on a more personal level, after our initial introduction as part of the Academy of Music scene.

As I originally wrote in "*UFOs Among The Stars - Close Encounters of The Famous*" (Global Communications): "Walli was known widely as the White Witch Of New York. Because of her contacts in the music industry, she had established quite an eclectic clientele for whom she would offer spiritual guidance and occasional good luck or love spells, always of a positive nature. She didn't dabble in black magick or even gris-gris (a New Orleans form of 'gray magick' that incorporates poppets and the use of talismans kept in a personal mojo bag). Walli was lively, imaginative, energetic, well spoken, and quite attractive in her flowing garments complete with fashionable silver moon adornments. Oh did I forget to mention long black hair, complete with dyed green streak highlights? Indeed, Wallie made a very bold fashion and occult statement wherever she went."

THE MAN WHO FELL TO EARTH

From what Walli told me and from what I pieced together on my own, early in life, Bowie had established his interest in all matters extraterrestrial. As a Brit teenager, David had helped edit a flying saucer newsletter. He admitted to me that he loved science fiction and was fascinated with life in space and the possibility that quite a few cosmic visitors had ended up on our earthly shores.

During a conversation, Bowie had gone out on a limb revealing that he had once had a close encounter. In the book "*Laugh Gnostic*," author Peter Koening paraphrases what Bowie said: "A friend and I were traveling in the English countryside when we both noticed a strange object hovering above a field. From then on, I have come to take this phenomenon seriously. I believe that what I saw was not the actual object but a projection of my own mind trying to make sense of this quantum topological doorway into dimensions beyond our own. It's as if our dimension is but one among an infinite number of others."

In the February 1975 issue of the long defunct "*CREEM Magazine*," Bowie seems to admit to a reporter that he might have an implant or metal inside his body. It's hard to define his exact feeling on this, but this is the quote attributed to him by Bruno Stein, the writer who conducted the interview:

"Well, it turned out David was in luck. If he went to a little town in Missouri at a certain time, he would be able to see in a seemingly empty field a fully equipped flying saucer repair shop at work.

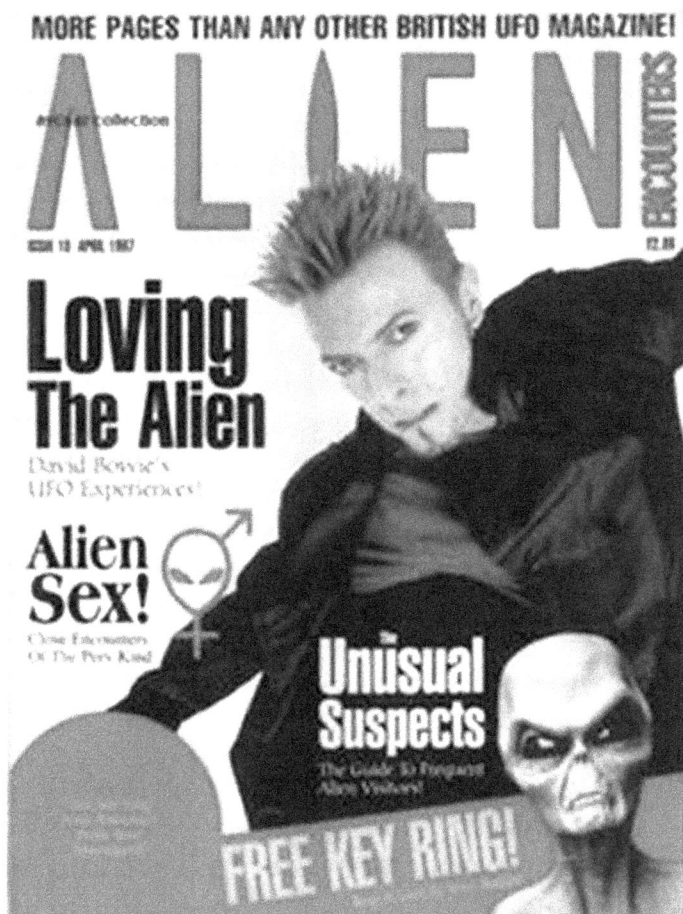

Even the UFO press couldn't contain themselves when it came to Bowie's flying saucer emissions.

"It was one of those fascinating things you learn at a Bowie soiree. This evening the gathering was rather intimate. There was Corinne, David's charming personal secretary, who ducked out early due to exhaustion (although another participant gossiped that she had someone interesting waiting for her in her hotel room). "I used to work for two guys who put out a UFO magazine in England," he told the flying saucer man. "About six years ago. And I made sightings six, seven times a night for about a year when I was in the observatory. We had regular cruises that came over. We knew the 6.15 was coming in and would meet up with another one. And they would be stationary for about half an hour, and then after verifying what they'd been doing that day, they'd shoot off.

"But, I mean, it's what you do with the information. We never used to tell anybody. It was beautifully dissipated when it got to the media. Media control is still based in the main on cultural manipulation. It's just so easy to do. When you set up one set of objectives toward the public and you've given them a certain definition for each code word, you hit them with the various code words and they're not going to believe anything if you don't want them to..."

From his performances, you could tell that nothing was too "non-establishment" for David. He incorporated time machines and space capsules into his act and wrote "A Space Oddity" and talked about how a "Starman" would like to come and visit us, "but he thinks he'd blow our minds." He appeared in the motion picture "The Man Who Fell To Earth," which has become a classic. In concert, Bowie was radiant and his fans were floating on a cloud, but behind the scenes an ominous specter was forming from which the master of time and space would quickly need some righteous assistance in order to escape a wall of paranoia that was building around him.

AND ALONG COMES MR. SCRATCH

Like many rockers before and after, David had taken a liking to the good life. You know the old adage: sex, drugs and rock and roll. Well, on top of this, add a heap of consciousness expansion and an interest in the occult and you will have the prevalent influences on what might have seemed like Bowie's immortal being.

But paranoia soon struck in the form of the ole nemesis "nose candy," commonly known as cocaine. With the help of Bowie himself and some close associates at the time, Marc Spitz details in *Bowie: A Biography*" (Crown) how David was living in L.A. just a few houses away from the estate where Charlie Manson's gang had terribly mutilated Sharon Tate and her friends in a ritualistic murder. Bowie had taken to doing blow regularly and was getting more and more desperate and paranoid with each passing day.

In a number of shocking revelations, biographer Marc Spitz explains precisely what was transpiring in the pop singer's troubled life: "While planning the follow-up to 'Young Americans,' Bowie would sit in the house with a pile of high-quality cocaine atop the glass coffee table, a sketch pad and a stack of books. '*Psychic Self Defense*' (Dion Fortune) was his favorite. Its author describes the book as a 'safeguard for protecting yourself against paranormal malevolence.'

"Using this and more arcane books on witchcraft, white magic and its malevolent counterpart, black magic, as rough guides to his own rapidly fragmenting psyche, Bowie began drawing protective pentagrams on every surface."

Bowie told the author, "I'd stay up for weeks. Even people like Keith Richards were floored by it. And there were pieces of me all over the floor.
I paid with the worst manic depression of my life. My psyche went through

the roof; it just fractured into pieces. I was hallucinating 24 hours a day."

Spitz adds, "Increasingly Bowie was convinced there were witches after his semen. They were intent on using it to make a child to sacrifice to the devil, essentially the plot to Roman Polanski's 1968 supernatural classic *'Rosemary's Baby.'*"

Seeing that he was in desperate need, the poet and songwriter with the beautiful red hair, Cherry Vanilla hooked Bowie up with Walli, who Spitz describes as a "Manhattan-based intellectual...who taught classes at the New York School of Occult Arts and Sciences, then located on Fourteenth Street, just north of Greenwich Village." (As mentioned, I ran the school, which began in the mid-1960s and thrived for more than a decade, promoting lectures and classes by the who's who of paranormal and UFO experts of that era, including Cleve Backster, Stanley Krippner, Jim Moseley, John Keel - and, of course our favorite White Witch.)

As added confirmation of the madness David was trying to cope with, ex-wife Angie Bowie reveals even more details of his fascination and dabbling into the occult in her own personal remembrance, *"Backstage Passes: Life on the Wild Side With David Bowie."*

"There was a beautiful Art Deco house on six acres, an exquisite site property and a terrific value at just $300,000, but he took one look at a detail I hadn't noticed, a hexagram painted on the floor of a circular room by the previous owner, Gypsy Rose Lee.

"A great deal of coddling and reassurance got us through that crisis, and I went and found the Doheny Drive house. Built in the late fifties or early sixties, it was a white cube surrounding an indoor swimming pool. David liked the place, but I thought it was too small to meet our needs for very long, and I wasn't crazy about the pool. In my experience, indoor pools are always a problem.

"This one was no exception, albeit not in any of the usual ways. Its drawback was one I hadn't encountered before and haven't seen or heard of since: Satan lived in it. With his own eyes, David said, he'd seen HIM rising up out of the water one night."

Feeling demonic forces moving in, David felt strongly that he needed an exorcism and asked that his newfound friend, white witch Walli Elmlark,

Street level view of home whose pool was possibly possessed by a demon.

be called upon to lend her assistance to remove the evil from his surroundings.

"A Greek Orthodox Church in L.A. would have done it for us (there was a priest available for such a service, the people had told me), but David wouldn't have it. No strangers allowed, he said. So there we stood, with just Walli's instructions and a few hundred dollars' worth of books, talismans, and assorted items from Hollywood's comprehensive selection of fine occult emporium.

"There he (David Bowie) was, then, primed and ready. The proper books and doodads were arranged on a big old-fashioned lectern. The incantation began, and although I had no idea what was being said or what language it was being said in, I couldn't stop a weird cold feeling rising up in me as David droned on and on.

"There's no easy or elegant way to say this, so I'll just say it straight. At a certain point in the ritual, the pool began to bubble. It bubbled vigorously (perhaps 'thrashed' is a better term) in a manner inconsistent with any explanation involving air filters or the like."

The rock and roll couple watched in amazement. Angie says she tried to be flippant - "'Well, dear, aren't you clever? It seems to be working.

Something's making a move, don't you think?' - but I couldn't keep it up. It was very, very strange; even after my recent experiences I was having trouble accepting what my eyes were seeing."

Angie said that she would peek through the glass doors which lead to the pool every so often and was dumbfounded by what she saw.

"On the bottom of the pool was a large shadow, or stain, which had not been there before the ritual began. It was in the shape of a beast of the underworld; it reminded me of those twisted, tormented gargoyles screaming silently from the spires of medieval cathedrals. It was ugly, shocking, and malevolent; it frightened me.

"I backed away from it, feeling very strange, went through the doorway, and told David what I'd seen, trying to be nonchalant but not doing very well. He turned white but eventually became revived enough to spend the rest of the night doing coke. He wouldn't go near the pool, though.

"I still don't know what to think about that night. It runs directly counter to my pragmatism and my everyday faith in the integrity of the 'normal' world, and it confuses me greatly. What troubles me the most is that if you were to call that stain the mark of Satan, I don't see how I could argue with you.

"David, of course, insisted that we move from the house as quickly as possible, and we did that, but I've heard from reliable sources (Michael Lipman for one, the property's real estate agent) that subsequent tenants haven't been able to remove the shadow. Even though the pool has been painted over a number of times, the shadow always comes back."

THE DARK SIDE OF THE OCCULT AND NAZISM

Bowie freely admitted that he was drawn at a point in his life to the darker side of the occult. He had expressed interest in the works of Aleister Crowley who the press was fond of calling "the wickedest man in the world," and dubbed the Anti-Christ. Crowley was said to be a Satanist which he wasn't. As part of his occult studies, Bowie read up on the O.T.O. - the Order of the Golden Dawn - an occult fraternal group heavily into sex magick. Bowie's favorite occult author was said to be Dion Fortune who

Bowie's Aleister Crowley influences are showing in this comparison pose.

David was reportedly reading Tarot Cards (using the Crowley deck) drawing symbols on the wall and pentagrams on the floor. Some say he heard voices, but that might have just been the whisperings of the cocaine. One visitor to his LA aBodē said that she had never seen such a massive pile of the white powder on anyone's coffee table (remember the stuff cuts well on a glass top!).

The Starman was also taken by the Kabbalah, a Hebrew form of mysticism, which might not have been so unusual considering that his mom was half Irish and half Jewish. As part of his studies he cast a huge Tree of Life symbol before him on a canvas. Author Peter Koening summed up Bowie's occult obsession thus: "Rumor has it that Bowie kept his hair and fingernail clippings in the fridge of Michael Lippman's home where he was living then, so they could not fall into the hands of those he thought wished to put spells on him. Bowie constructed an altar in the living room and he graced the walls with various magick symbols which he hand painted. Candles burned around the clock, he regularly performed banishing rituals, and he protected his friends by drawing sigils on their hands."

The devil pool was not to be David Bowie's last encounter with the paranormal.

In an interview with "*Uncut*" magazine, Bowie producer Tony Visconti discussed reports that Chateaud 'Herouville, near Paris, where "*Low*" was recorded in 1976, was haunted. "There was certainly some strange energy in that chateau." On the first day David took one look at the master bedroom and said, 'I'm not sleeping in there!' He took the room next door. The master bedroom had a very dark corner, right next to the window, ironically, that seem to just suck light into it. It was colder in that corner too. I took the bedroom because I wanted to test my meditation abilities. I never admitted this"

One cannot omit the fact that David was intrigued by the occult influences on Hitler and the Nazi party. He had read the book "*The Morning of the Magicians*," in his search to find out about the Holy Grail and the Sword of Destiny which by owning it Hitler might become the most powerful man in the world.

As stated, Walli and I worked for a number of years on several projects and even co-authored a book together. Out of print for decades, once in a while I still run across a copy of "*Rock Raps of the Seventies*," offered on e-bay or elsewhere at an exorbitant price.

I believe that from his encounters with Walli the rock star found it much easier than it should have been to kick his cocaine habit due to her spell casting and positive affirmations.

Somehow, I can't deny the possibility that Walli looked down from time to time and perhaps sang along with David Bowie as he performed all over the world in concert. Long recovered from drugs and the dark aspects of occultism, he went about raising a family and going on with his chosen task of climbing the ladder of pop star success.

Over the years we had heard unsubstantiated rumors that Bowie was intrigued by an incident where a UFO was said to have crashed in the desert. We were never able to pin anything down about this incident until we found out that it was actually scribed by Bowie's original publicist and a longtime friend of ours, Cherry Vanilla, who was in his hotel suite when the story came over the TV. Writing under Bowie's name, this is what the fiery redhead is quoting as having been said under Bowie's name in "*Mirabelle*," a sort of diary published by Bowie's camp.

"I heard the most incredible thing the other day that I must tell you about, and I promise every single word of it is true! I was in Detroit, where I was due to do a concert, and before the show I was sitting in my hotel room listening to the radio.

"Suddenly, the newsman interrupted the regular program with the news that a spaceship had been found in the desert - an alien spaceship about six feet wide and thirty feet long - and inside were three alien beings. The three creatures were killed on impact when the spaceship plummeted to Earth, but they were taken to a hospital to be examined

David adds to the Tree of Life symbol on the floor before him.

anyway. These people looked like human beings but were much smaller and, when they were examined, it was discovered that their vital organs were like human beings too! The catch is that their brains were found to be much farther advanced! Wow!

"As soon as the newscast was over, I got all the band and my back-up singers together and had them ring up radio and TV stations all over the country to see if they had all got the report. About half the stations said they had and half denied it. So, it really is quite a mystery. No one knows what's happened to the spaceship or the spacemen at this point, and it seems that someone is trying to cover up the whole matter completely!"

And so it goes.

David Bowie died of cancer leaving a great void in the musical world and in the daily lives of his devoted fans.

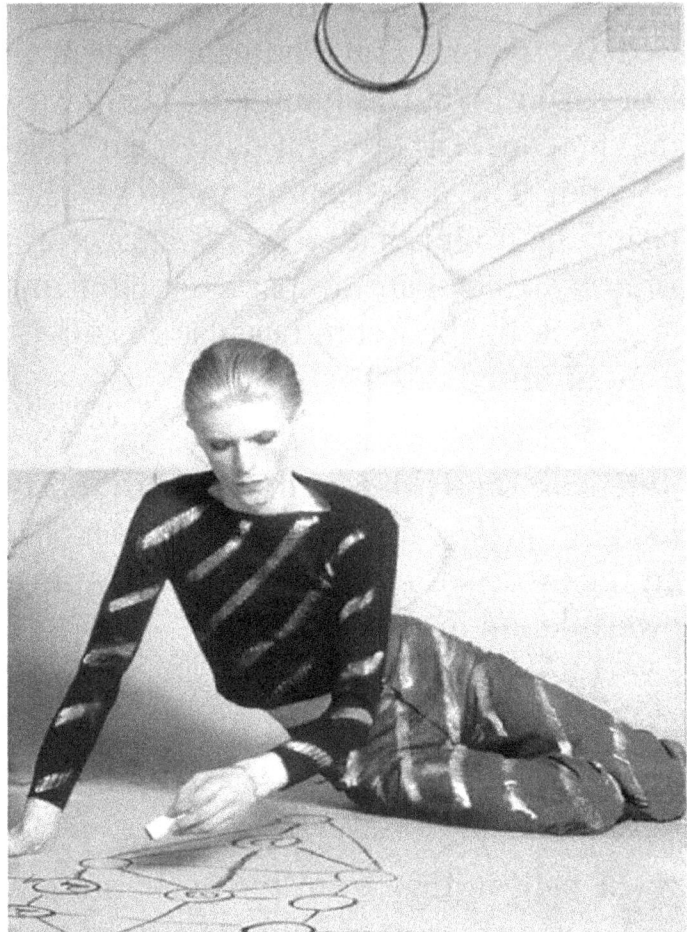

Toward his last days he became more of a private person than ever before living with his wife and daughter in Greenwich Village. There are some who say that his last song "*Blackstar*," was "visionary," dealing with the arrival of the mysterious Planet X which could lead to the destruction of the earth. Let us hope this is only a science fiction scenario that Bowie drew upon and not a prophecy of some devastation to befall our planet.

We really need Walli and David back here now. It would seem that their given undertaking is far from over!

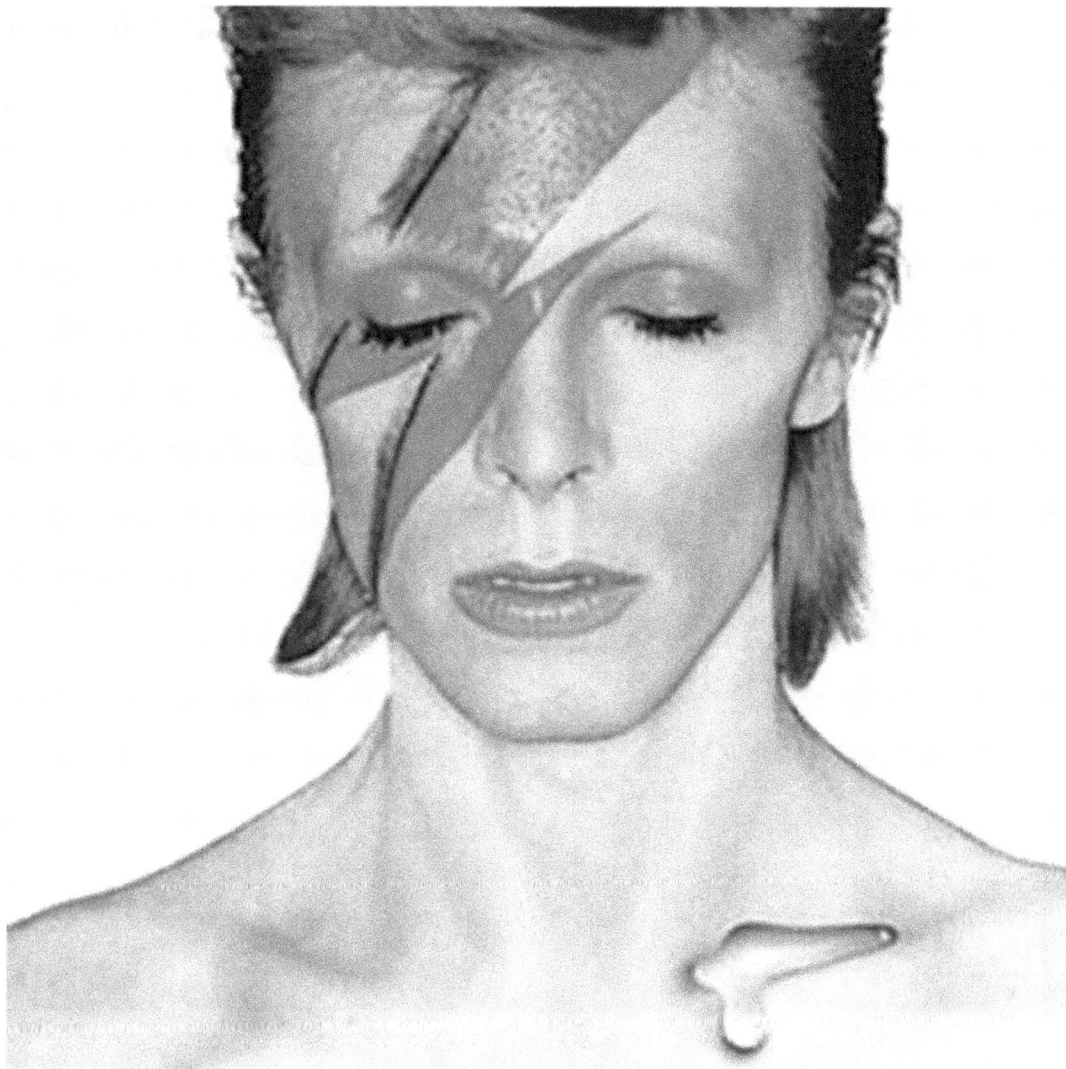

Bowie as Ziggy Stardust.

Carol Ann Rodriguez depicts the rebirth of universal souls as inspired by Walli's belief that many musicians were being "reincarnated here" as part of a cosmic plan.

3.

THE PRINCIPLES OF THE CRAFT

AS the "principal" of the New York School of Occult Arts and Sciences, even though I knew a lot about the arcane and esoteric through my own mystical experiences, I was learning something new every day it seems. Such as the meaning of the popular Wiccan term Blessed Be, which in the slang of the craft simply means "take care," and that blessings have been bestowed upon you by the Goddess Diana.

It was the early 1970s, while running one of the first metaphysical centers in the country; I noticed some of those in attendance at the lectures and workshops were more serious minded in their studies than others.

You had a percentage who wanted to find their soul mate through almost any means possible, such as having a love spell cast for them or applying attraction oil behind their ear lobe, or even finding out the different types of herbs that could be used as an aphrodisiac. Others came hoping to attract prosperity into their lives by wearing a talisman for that purpose, one that would manifest them a fancy new car or a big home in the bergs. Another group wished to remain youthful forever or on the extreme side to obtain immortality – we did have a female "vampire" on the premises if that would help any. Someone once tripped over her coffin during a séance held in the dark in the back part of the occult center's loft and fell directly on top of her. They were lucky they didn't end up with a stake through their heart. Witch Hazel – yes that was her real name, she had it changed legally and it was even on her driver's license which she showed me – played with the "dark side" of the occult. Certainly she was not a Walli-type Wiccan that was quite obvious as she would enter the school sporting a flaring black cape. She did have a wicked sense of humor and everyone loved her, though I'm not sure how much she loved them back. Damn I miss those days!

There was another group who came to the study center for spiritual enlightenment. These I guess you could classify as the more "serious students." They sought out more than superficial cognition. They were seeking the true "wisdom of the ages," a degree of knowledge that would have lasting benefit. They took notes and they asked questions.

In regular attendance was a young lady who traveled from one of the outer boroughs, got off the train at Union Square and walked over the few blocks to take a seat in one of the front rows of folding chairs which overlooked a giant picture window that faced toward Seventh Avenue and its heavy foot traffic made up mainly of shoppers, and local residents making their way home from hum drum office jobs uptown. There was only one little sign at the bottom of the stairs so that unless this was your final destination for the evening, the New York School of Occult Arts and Sciences was pretty much "our little secret."

"Bad" witch, good witch. Witch Hazel and Walli strike a fetching pose at the NY School of Occult Arts and Sciences before one of our many workshops on witchcraft. Hazel wasn't opposed to dabbling in the dark arts if the occasion arose.
Photo by Tim Beckley

Carol Ann roomed with Walli for several years.

Carol Ann Rodriguez was in her twenties and says she had been into the occult for some time. "While in my teens I picked up books by Brad Steiger and John Keel, among others. I also found a book titled 'The Fundamentals of Yoga' and found that the breathing exercises recommended by the author triggered astral experiences and vivid dreams. I had just begun to read books about Wicca when I saw an advertisement in the 'Village Voice' and decided to attend a lecture on witchcraft at the Occult Center run by Tim Beckley. It seemed like it might be a strange place so naturally I was a bit apprehensive about going somewhere I had heard that the place might be full of Satanists or black magicians." Though while contributing to this book, Carol finally admitted she was just trying to get my goat (the goat being the symbol of the horned God that some witch-crafters worship as the male deity), that she had no reason to believe we were being overrun by those of the left hand path.

As it turns out, according to her own admission, Carol had nothing to be apprehensive. The black magicians and Satanists were actually operating across town and were in reality a rather affable group who never tortured anyone or sacrifice animals. Maybe they were holding a couple of naked sex orgies in someone's loft, but each to their own.

After attending Walli's lecture, Carol felt totally at ease. "I liked Walli's wonderful way of explaining witchcraft and paganism as a positive way of life and decided to sign up for one of Walli's classes which she held at her apartment uptown."

DO ONTO OTHERS

In her classes Walli explained the basics of her faith. "Wicca is about love and worshiping. Notice I didn't mention sex - although that's nice too, we're not weird!

"The only 'don't' we practice is don't harm others. If we do harm to anyone else, the next basic belief would take care of whatever 'nasty' we propagated. That is the belief in being reborn and having to go through 'training' all over again. Furthermore, whatever deed you do could backfire on you and come back two or even three fold."

THE GODDESS

Walli emphasized that witches do not believe in heaven or hell. "There is no god seated on a throne in the clouds and no hell to descend to. There are low level spirits known as elementals or demons which can attach themselves to humans who might have low self esteem or who indulge in harmful activities. There is, however, a Great Mother or the Goddess Diana as she has been named. She was formed out of an infinite void creating an energy source which no religion can tell you how or when it originated.

"Diana is symbolized by the Moon and only silver jewelry should be worn by true witches, as this strengthens their ties with the Godhead. Diana had a 'brother' known as Lucifer who has nothing to do with the Devil or Satan, both of whom are an invention of Christianity. He is the bearer of light and knowledge and is symbolized by the Sun. The belief is that Diana fell madly in love with Lucifer, but he wanted no part of her. One time she turned herself into the form of a white cat, and in this form gained entrance to his bed. Once settled where she had longed to be, she returned to human form and coupled with him. From this union came a daughter known as Aradia who was sent to earth in mortal form to teach the ways of Magick. She taught healing, the use of herbs, various spells and the Wiccan way of life, which is followed to this day."

WICCAN HOLY DAYS

While some witches might observe the more customary religious holidays like Easter, Christmas and Chanukah for the sake of their friends or families, in Wicca there are four major Sabbaths and four minor Sabbaths which are uniformly celebrated.

"The major Sabbaths are All Hallows Eve, October 31 - best known as Halloween by 'outsiders.' This is the highest holiday of all for us.

"Candlemass, Feburary 2.

"Beltane, May Eve.

"Lammas, August 2.

"Then there are the minor Sabbats which fall on the spring and autumn equinoxes and the summer and winter solstices."

There are also a variety of Esbats which occur at each full moon. "Most witches," notes Walli, "feel since power is the greatest at that time of each month this is when the covens are to gather. A coven is a group of witches akin to a closely knit clan not to exceed

A version of the Wiccan Calendar with its Sabbaths.

twelve members plus the High Priestess or High Priest but possibly consisting of fewer initiates. Together they can merge their magickal powers in one united force assisting in making the total energy level higher and thus enabling the coven to accomplish greater tasks than one person might be able to accomplish working alone."

In an introduction to a serious of short lessons Walli put into booklet form, I added my own two cents on the growing popularity in the occult and in Wicca in particular. "Hundreds of thousands of new devotes, many of them young people," I pointed out, "are fleeing from more orthodox faiths in the hopes of finding something of a more personal spiritual value. Their search has led them to the 'Old Religion,' known as Witchcraft or more simply Wicca-the religion of the wise." I extended my thoughts with the comment that, "Witchcraft is becoming the religion of the New Age. Astrologers and prophets have long told us that in this Age of Aquarius our psychic abilities and knowledge of occult practices will be enhanced greatly. Some people will even develop to the stage where they will be able to read

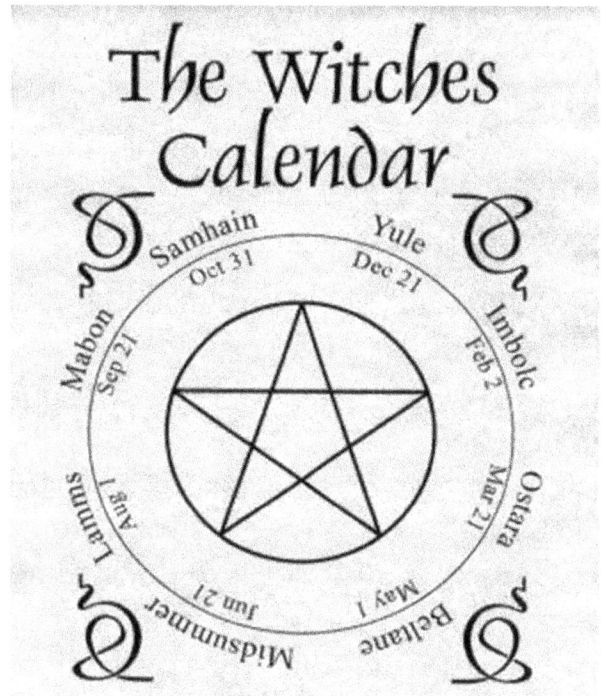

minds and communicate telepathically."

Carol is a fantastic intuitive artist. Her "spacey graphics" remind me somewhat of the spirited "psychedelic" creations of Peter Max, utilizing brilliant colors with landscapes of rainbows and stars. Her unique water colors often depict the pagan moon and sun gods and there is little doubt that Carol Ann must have been influenced by Walli's lectures and private workshops. She peppered the white witch of New York with questions on all matters concerning the occult and Wiccan philosophy. If you haven't noticed, Carol's art is scattered throughout the pages of this book. Walli told her work would be in demand.

Some of the beliefs Walli taught included the following topics:

WHAT EXACTLY IS THE WICCAN WAY OF LIFE?

"It is not easy to tie together the threads of Wicca, but it is safe to say that it is more a way of life than a do and don't, hell and brimstone, religion. Probably the most comprehensive method would be to state our beliefs. Our beliefs relate to a total acceptance and understanding of many things that upset and baffle so many outside this mystical faith."

WE DO NOT BELIEVE IN A GOD OR DEVIL

"We each have the 'god' potential within us. This is what we are striving for in our incarnations. As for a devil, we absolutely have no belief in him, nor do we believe in Beelzebub or any of the other charming creatures that people so often say we worship."

WE DO BELIEVE IN SPIRIT GUIDES!

"We have help available to us all the time. Unfortunately most people are so busy plotting out how to make more money or jamming up their heads with worry (a useless expenditure of energy) or (horrors) seeking retribution or revenge upon others, that they block out the help that's offered. Witches can be infuriating to their co-workers and acquaintances. In the midst of a crisis they stay calm to the point of probably appearing unconcerned.

"This is far from true. It's just that every witch knows the answer will be shown to her. All they have to do is keep their minds clear and wait. While everyone around them has shorted their spirit circuits by panic and fear, the witch leaves a clear channel open ready to hear the advice of her or his Spirit Guides."

EVERYTHING HAPPENS FOR A REASON

"The second part of the perennial calm is the absolute belief that everything happens as it should. There is a reason for everything. Looking back over your life, is it not true that from every situation you thought was a calamity, from every love affair gone down the drain, either a great lesson is learned or the situation thought to be such a loss at the time would have been a bad mistake. The reason may not always be apparent. Sometimes it takes years to see the reason why something had to happen as it did, but there is always a reason. Really seeing that these concepts are true immediately eases situations that would have built incredible anxiety and energy loss.

"Did you miss the last train to that special weekend? We might be disappointed but we would shrug and say 'I wasn't meant to go.' Have you encountered a number of mysterious coincidences leading to a great new friend or job? We do not believe in coincidence. Things happen the way they are supposed to happen."

WHAT ABOUT FREE WILL?

"Again, things happen the way they are supposed to happen, and help is available to you ONLY if you are willing to stay open enough to see the way when it's shown to you.

"Your life is set up to offer the opportunities you need to progress. In each given circumstance you have the choice (free will) of how to handle the given problem."

Part of Walli's Wiccan belief system included what I would call "human relationship building." She put a great deal of emphasis on how one should treat and expect to be treated by other individuals in an honest and forthright manner. In short one should not lie or even exaggerate the truth, as this only ends up producing bad karma that will inadvertently come back to haunt you.

DO NOT LIE OR PLAY HEAD GAMES

"There is always a shock when first we learn the rest of the world thinks and acts differently than we do. We don't understand the necessity to lie. It's a waste of time and a lot of trouble to have to remember who you told what to. If you have done nothing to hide there is no necessity to conceal the truth. Very simple."

WHAT ABOUT A WHITE LIE?

"The term white lie bothers me. A lie is a lie IS a lie. We don't lie! We would not go out of our way to tell a friend her dress is horrendous, however, if that friend asks our opinion, that is exactly what she will get. If the dress looked awful on her, what kind of a friend would we be to say it looked great? If she didn't want to know the truth, why did she ask what we thought? It is NEVER kind to lie. You NEVER in the long run 'save' someone's feelings. Omitting truth, by the way, is just as much a lie as a spoken lie. Did you omit to tell your girlfriend your ex dropped into the office just at lunchtime and pushed you into taking her out for a hamburger?"

Some might think this concept to be a bit harsh or extreme. I'll leave that up to you to decide as Walli expands on some of her more philosophic sensitivity.

FEELINGS WE DON'T FEEL

"I have been expressing my thoughts on the Wiccan faith and I have been trying to stay within those guidelines, although separating a witch from her magick is almost impossible. At this point a bit should be mentioned about white magick vs. black magick. Here again, popular misconceptions have tossed us all into the same magickal cauldron. Not true. The white witch does ONLY good, no hexes, no toad turnings. As a matter of fact, the white witch has very little choice in the matter. To do harm in magick there are certain emotions that must come into play.

Hatred, revenge, greed, to give an idea, are emotions that true followers of Wicca should never feel."

ISN'T HATRED AND REVENGE UNIVERSAL EMOTIONS?

"If one truly, truly understands Wicca it totally demolishes these unrewarding emotions. Either you have learned to go beyond your own feelings and understand why someone has performed a hateful act towards you, or you realize the life plane of that individual is so low that he just doesn't know any better. Would you hate a baby for spilling his milk? With understanding, hate must go. As for revenge, we know only too well we need do nothing. If someone has done harm it will return to him three-fold with no help from us. If we could send a "nasty" back, all we would be doing in the long run, would be evil to ourselves."

WE WERE MEANT TO BE GIVERS AND HEALERS

"We used to heal the sick, help the crops, and mix up a little something to help the needy. Times have changed (notice I don't say 'progressed'), but those basic instincts to give, to heal have not. Speaking for myself, the healing takes the form of taking people instantly off drug freaks, mopping up blood and escorting accident cases to New York Hospital (my favorite Emergency Room). I have opened my house, given my clothes away, fed and mothered those I have tried to help. I will allow people to use me for awhile, but if they do not start to learn, then out they go. I have finally learned I cannot help the entire world. If one won't learn, there are others who will. I will spend my time on them."

THE MEANING OF LOVE

In her personal life, Walli placed a great deal of emphasis on love which shows through in her teachings.

"I have said it before and I will say it again: the world does a lot of talking about love and truth but in fact knows little about it. Love to us means thinking beyond ourselves to the other person. What might be best for me might not be best for him. His interests come first. I feel hurt at something he's done. Instead of just reacting to "I'm hurt," we say first,

"Why did he do this? Did I inadvertently hurt him? Is he just unaware? Is there something else bothering him that has manifested itself this way?" Then we try to talk about it and work it out quietly and calmly. It is not always easy."

But as Carol Ann Rodriguez surely would agree Walli was not so much trying to convert anyone to Wicca, but was more into spreading the "true gospel" about witchcraft and its positive side. "She wanted to dispel the accusations that witches were devil worshipers who preformed blood sacrifices." Carol says she truly feels Walli wanted to use her powers – and she did have them – in a positive way, "to help others when she possibly could."

Walli © The Helen Hovey Collection.

4.

THE WORLD OF WICCA, SPIRIT GUIDES AND LIFE IN THE HEREAFTER

WALLI, and that implies Wiccans in general, held a strong belief in the world of spirit, that there is life after death and that spirit guides exist in another reality who can help us out in times of personal need. The closest to this theology would be in the tenants of spiritualism minus the trappings of the Christian bindings which say that Jesus will meet you at the pearly gate and that you will float on a cloud and play the harp for eternity (hell no we like rock and roll!).

Witches believe spirit guides are all around and can help in times of need.

WHAT HAPPENS WHEN WE DIE?

What happens when we die and what does it feel like? Walli has it all figured out.

"There is no pain in death. Perhaps in the dying, but not in death. We retain the individuality of the life just past. Memory retention is complete. However, additional knowledge is acquired. You become aware of the problems that were to be resolved. You then set up your next life in such a way that you will give yourself the opportunity to resolve these problems. Once you are reborn, memory of all previous lives cease (except for those few glimpses of déjà vu) and when the actual problem does arise, you, in your new mortal body, have the choice of free will to exercise. It is at this time that you will either handle the problems appropriately and gain spiritually or blunder once again.

"Since you do set up your own forthcoming life you usually set it up in such a manner that will enable you to meet again those people you loved and were very close with before. Have you ever met someone you feel quite at home with, someone you feel you've been friends with for years?

AND WHAT ABOUT SPIRIT GUIDES

As for the existence of spirit guides - similar to guardian angels, though they could be non mortals having never lived on earth or most probably departed loved ones hanging around to be of assistance when called upon - Walli plots it out this way.

"There are those spirits who wish to become spirit guides and watch over those they have loved on earth. We all have spirit guides. Have you ever heard a little voice in your head reminding you of something you forgot? The older generation used to call this their 'conscious' when referring to speaking to them.

"We of the Wiccan belief are quite sure that these voices in our head are quite real and should be listened to. Throughout history these voices have nudged us by 'whispering in our ear,' or providing us with mental images to follow. Some have spoken openly of such occurrences (such as members of the spiritualist community who communicate with the spirit world through mediums at a séance) though Joan of Arc should have

When not hanging out at Yankee stadium "The Babe" (Ruth) was living in one of the upper floors of the Ansonia just off Broadway.

probably kept her mouth shut you might say.

"There are some spirits," Walli explains who take the bull by the horn and willing return to "the misery of the earth plane, being sent back here in mortal form to heal, to help and teach the masses, who grope blindly seeking 'answers' and 'happiness' on a material level."

One can rightfully assume that these are some of the musicians like Bowie and Bolan and Hendrix who heal through their music and their message.

But do these "messengers" know who they are?

"Usually, for many years, they are relatively unaware of what they are and what their mission is. They all seem to have the same tale to tell: an essentially lonely and alone childhood, feeling somewhat apart and different, trying to help with problems, hating violence, not understanding the lying and the game playing of the people in their lives.

Walli felt it was her spiritual duty to inform those blessed with this task what their purpose in life was all about. That is why she continually attempted to make contact and establish a relationship with those musicians and entertainers who had been "placed here," but not made aware of the circumstances surrounding their arrival back on the earth plane. Her position as a rock writer, her glamorous look and sensuality and her ability to teach the principles of WICCA in a sane and rational way allowed her the opportunity to bring into manifestation her desires - but hey that's what witchcraft is all about!

WALLI GOES TO A SÉANCE

In order to communicate with the spirit world and its arsenal of helpful guides Walli would attend séances from time to time. Carol Ann Rodriguez had started rooming with Ms Elmlark in an apartment just off Central Park and together they would enjoy attending services at the Universalist Spiritualist Church.

"The church," Carol reminisces as she sat across from me, was located inside the once stately, but deteriorating Ansonia Hotel (Babe Ruth had once resided there) located on the upper west side of Manhattan just off Broadway. "Walli and I would attend services there given by an individual the Rev Clifford Bias, whom I believe to be an above average, if not a great, medium."

Clifford Bias organized a magical study group known as the Ancient Mystical Order of Seekers (A.M.O.S.) and he wrote and published a series of A.M.O.S. books, including "The Probationer." Both Walli and Carol would go to him for readings on a regular basis.

For whatever it is worth, a quick Google provides this rather one-sided, rather inflammatory, tidbit on both the Ansonia and the Reverend. "...the ramshackle Ansonia began to attract as tenants, for indefinable reasons, all sorts of mediums, psychics, spiritualists, and fortune-tellers. A Dr. Clifford Bias began holding quasi-religious services in a chapel off the lobby on Sunday afternoons. One week, Dr. Bias was blindfolded and summoning up the dead when the great singer Geraldine Farrar appeared to deliver the message, 'The Ansonia isn't what it used to be when I was there.'"

"Walli and I felt that Mr. Bias and the others at the church did the best psychic readings. I also attended classes there on the Tarot and Kabbalah. Walli told me that Bias was her teacher and suggested I get a reading done by him. It was the summer of 1973 and I was hoping he could help me on my path. I knew that Walli was a really good psychic, so I could hardly wait to see what Rev. Bias had to say."

Carol says her anticipation was well founded. "He gave me one of the best, most accurate readings I ever had, or ever would have. Rev. Bias first told me not to call him Rev Bias, to call him Clifford, or if I thought he was too old and decrepit to be called by his first name, I may call him Mr. Bias. He described my deceased father and said he was my spirit guide. He knew I had been interested in art as a child and said that interest would be renewed. He said I would get a job using my hands. It would be a job, job, but it would reveal something that was hidden, a great creative talent."

"Arlington Operated"

Hotel Ansonia

Broadway, 73rd to 74th Streets,   New York City

12 minutes from Penn. & Grand Central Stations
5 minutes to Theatres & Shopping District

1260 ROOMS
(All Outside)

New York's most complete hotel. Everything for comfort and convenience of our guests.

Two Restaurants
Open from 6.30 A. M. until midnight

Music : : Dancing
2 Radio Orchestras
Ladies Turkish Bath
Beauty Parlor
Drug Store
Barber Shop
Stock Brokers Office
All in the Ansonia Hotel

TRANSIENT RATES

300 Rooms and Bath ....$3.50 per day
Large double Rooms, twin beds, Bath ....$6.00 per day
Parlor Bedroom & Bath (2 persons) ......$7.00 per day

Special Weekly and Monthly Rates

A restful hotel—away from all the noise and "dirt" of the "Roaring Forties." No coal smoke, our steam plant equipped oil fuel. Coolest Hotel in New York in Summer.

The Ansonia

In Conjunction with the Hotels Colonial, Anderson, Richmond & Cosmopolitan
"Arlington Operated"

$7 a day would get you a big room with a bath in the Ansonia Hotel along with a seance if you wandered into the parlor where the Spiritualist Church were holding their meetings.

Carol added that Clifford refused the fee for his reading, "saying he knew I didn't have a job." Carol eventually did get a job working in a city day care center and eventually at Tim Beckley's Inner Light/Global Communications publishing company. "I worked with my hands stuffing envelopes, answering correspondence, and helping to fill orders. But also I began to have more opportunities to do illustrations. I have done any number of book covers and even have my own art book. And there will soon be a Volume II of *'Carol's Fantastic Universe.'*"

Several times Carol and Walli attended séances which Clifford Bias conducted.

"The room would be dark and he would go into a trance and the spirits would start speaking through him. The first séance was the most memorable. My father came through saying he had my puppy there with him. I said 'Tricksey?' 'Ruff,' there came a loud bark and everyone laughed."

It's good to know that according to Walli you need not be, pardon the expression, "dead wood," once you have passed away.

Marc Bolan
Photo © Helen Hovey Collection Academy of Music

5.

MARC BOLAN - MERLIN IN
KING ARTHUR'S COURT

A POEM ESPECIALLY FOR YOU MARC BOLAN

We are pioneering in an age that's just begun.

In a time of thought continuum and space beyond the sun.

Where some acknowledge there is a spirit that is free

But most of the world are planes below and therefore cannot see

To speak at them of Priestesses and places just past Mars

Is only wasting energies, so speak to them of cars.

Speak to them of mortgages and tax rises

While teaching them of mind power in your "Pop Star" now disguise.

– Walli Elmlark

WALLI was particularly bewitched by Marc Bolan lead singer and glam master of the British band T-Rex.

Marc Bolan died in a car crash. He was born September 30, 1947, left us, September 16, 1977.

There was, she sensed, something "magickal" about him, in the true occult sense of the word, magick being spelled the Wiccan way - with the letter K at the end. To the White Witch's way of thinking Bolan's "supernatural vibe" went well beyond just the ethereal quality of his music. There was, she thought, something "on the far side of unique" about him. It wasn't just his persona, though that was certainly appealing to her, the way he dressed, the way he strutted about the stage, the way he threw his scarf about his neck like the Lord of the land. Bolan took to wearing top hats and feather boas, as well as, putting drops of glitter on each of his cheekbones.

Marc Bolan
Photo©Helen Hovey Collection

No it wasn't just his mannerisms that caught Walli's attention, but it was in what he had to say musically that drove her to the conclusion that he was born to be "special!" It had more to do, she explained about how he communicated and "what he said" to his young and enthusiastic fans.

BOLAN AS MERLIN THE MAGNIFICENT

"I think Marc was the 5th Century magician Merlin in a previous lifetime," Walli shocked me with her pronouncement. "Besides being a fantastic poetic-song writer, Marc – like the warlock from King Arthur's court – was a musical sorcerer, a prophet, a bard and an adviser to his legion of fans." It dawned on me during our conversation that the White Witch before me could have indeed known Bolan when he lived as Merlin "way back yonder in time," since the circumstances surrounding their lives were so similar.

Walli was a staunch believer in reincarnation; it was part of her Wiccan belief system. "There cannot be a believer in Wicca who can doubt the existence of reincarnation," she explained "It is the ground work on which our religion is build. We pay, either in this life or the next for the wrongs we commit. Life on the earth plane is only a school. We work our way up on the astral planes, of which there are seven, by returning over and over until we reach true spiritual enlightenment."

As part of this notion, Walli felt confident that certain individuals – specifically those with deep roots into the rock and roll community – were passing over into earthly bodies from other planets and astral planes to help raise the vibrations of the earth and contribute to the spiritual development

David Bowie and Marc Bolan Granada TV 1977.
Collinbell.org

of the planet. These individuals would include David Bowie, Jimi Hendrix and Marc Bolan who were turning on the "youngsters" with their radical messages of peace and love while most often including occult themes in their performances, such as Bowie with his Ziggy Stardust persona a spaceman fallen to earth.

One of Walli's missions was to convince a handful of musicians she met- the "chosen ones" - that they were part of this global program of enlightenment. At one point in her career, the witch flew to England with King Crimson's Robert Fripp to record a spoken word album. According to musician and Fripp biographer Sid Smith the album, "was called the *Cosmic Childen*." Side one consisting of Fripp and Elmark in conversation where she outlines her experiences and commitment to Wicca. On side two, she talks to DJ Jeff Dexter about cosmic children – spirits from other places who take physical forms such as Hendrix, Brian Eno, Bowie and Mike

Gibbons, drummer with Badfinger." At the time Fripp stated: "The function of the album is to reach out to the children like the drummer from Badfinger. I want to say, 'You're not nutty, you're not a freak because you can't related to what's around you.'"

Fripp and Elmlark were supposed to hook up with Bowie and Bolan in the UK. We don't know whether they ever did or not because the spoken word tapes – with musical interludes by these famous artists – have never surfaced and are believed to have been destroyed. To her friends and to members of the occult community they would be a very valuable item should anyone ever come across the "lost recording."

The album was discussed when Fripp gave an interview with Trouser Press's Ihor Slabicky in 1978:

"RF: The music for it was a 45-second piece by Eno on synthesizer which I did in a way that lasted about 20 minutes. I just repeated it time and time again and cross-faded it in places. Side one has a percussion solo by Frank Perry, who's a quite remarkable percussion player..."

To reassert, indeed, one of the things Walli was so convinced of was that many of the popular rock stars, so admired among the youth, were being reincarnated - or relocated - here on Earth at this specific time in order to bring about a beneficial change in our cultural attitudes. It's debatable as to the success of this program of

Marc Bolan
Photo © Helen Hovey Collection

reincarnated souls especially since the main champion for the program's cause is no longer with us.

THE MAN WITH THE TOP HAT

I know Walli used to be particularly enthralled with the "cosmic charm" of Marc Bolan, who many knew as the "Wizard." Said the White Witch about this glam artist who sang and played guitar with the band T. Rex: "I have had to meet hundreds of 'pop' stars, but it is a rare name that I can't wait to meet. Marc Bolan was one. I had gotten a very definite impression of what Marc's thinking would be like from listening to his lyrics. They are filled with allusions to wizards, priestesses, planet queens and other varied cosmic complexities."

Countless T. Rex songs written by Marc Bolan refer to flying saucers and outer space, including "*The Visit*," "*Ballrooms of Mars*," "*Space Boss*," "*Galaxy*" and "*Interstellar Soul*."

Years later I had the opportunity to speak with record producer Tony Visconti, whose greatest success was "*Electric Warrior*," the album that made T. Rex front man Marc Bolan a superstar and cemented Visconti's producing prowess. Visconti did nine T. Rex albums and also produced for David Bowie. I was hoping that perhaps Visconti knew the whereabouts of the master tapes to this very unusual record, or could at least clue me in on some of Marc Bolan's cosmic wisdom. And was it true that he was a sort of "Walk-In," a child of the cosmos?

"I can tell you for a fact that Marc wasn't into any of this magical stuff at all," Visconti said. He floored me with his comments, which were totally contradictory to what Walli would have had me believe.

Tony pooh-poohed the entire idea of a musical metaphysical metaphor. He shrugged off the entire concept, and I could see he just didn't want to be bothered with answering questions about UFOs, witchcraft, magic and the like. He could have at least mentioned that John Lennon's sighting of a UFO over the NYC skyline had taken place in the company of May Pang, Tony's one-time wife, who of course was standing near the former Beatle when the craft started to close in on their position on a balcony, sans clothing and with pizza in hand.

Still From Marc Bolan "The Wizard - Mini Movie" on YouTube.

Strange remarks indeed in view of the story Walli told about meeting Marc in his hotel room. Walli became convinced that "there was a side of Marc that millions never had seen, because it is outside of the realm of general understanding. The concept is so tremendous that it will take a great deal of time before the world is ready, but, right now, all around you are the teachers, the forerunners, the guides that have already begun their work.

"Jimi Hendrix is a prime example," Walli continued. "It is amazing how each of these cosmic teachers at one point had an encounter with Jimi. It was almost as if he travelled the planet hand-picking his people before he returned to that place in time somewhere beyond Mars from which he came."

A very wacky concept in the early and mid-1970s that has caught on with many New Agers today.

For a while, after seeing a live performance, Walli began to lose faith. Maybe Marc was not such a wizard after all as his monitors blew up and the sound system went haywire. But she had a meeting set up with Bolan in a couple of days and she wasn't about the cancel it!

Marc was late showing up for the interview, but, when he did return to his room after a whirlwind series of interviews set up with journalists all around the city, he flew into the place like a fireball.

"We went into a back room and I sat on the floor next to him," Walli recalled. "I listened to him try to explain to a large woman that none of us ever really die (naturally, we believe in reincarnation). He spoke of cosmic awareness, mind power, the fact that he spends a lot of time with gypsies 'because while they are not into formal schooling. They KNOW!'

"Our last five sentences came about when my photographer interrupted long enough to catch the last few leap-year day rays of light for pictures. 'I wish I could go insane or die at times,' I said. 'But I'm not allowed.'" (Walli did die by her own hand, tragically.)

"Of course you're not," Marc consoled her. "You are one of the children, you know that. We know we are all lonely, we must be. We live in a different place, but there is nothing to be done for it."

"Marc, there is a song on your album. It's the shortest song in there, but it gives me such strength. The words came at me like cryptic messages, a few days ago, when I really needed help to go on. I needed a sign that all we know is true, for at times we all wonder if we're just not totally mad. The song is 'Life's a Gas.' I had just thrown a whole group of people out of my life. They hadn't learned, and they were draining me. I hated to get rid of them, but I knew I had to and it would be all right. But I was very down. One hour later, I put on your record and heard, 'It doesn't really matter at all, no it really doesn't matter at all, life's a gas.' And I felt my strength returning. Was I right?"

Marc's eyes lit up and the magic poured through with its blinding brilliance.

"But of course! That's what the whole song's about! It doesn't matter at all. You must not let things matter. Things happen for a reason, and we can make them happen. There is nothing about my career that is an accident."

"We looked at each other and the understanding was total.

"My photographer kept saying, 'Look into the camera, Marc. Walli, please, look into the camera.' It was difficult. We are big on eyes. That is where the spirit, soul and heart come through. So much can be said when no words can be spoken. When we left, it was almost like a physical loss. There had been so little time. Yet, at the same time, I felt a tremendous gain. We had been together as if we were two people making love."

There were never to be any future meetings as Marc died prematurely on a winding road, perhaps traveling out of the body back to where Walli believed he came from.

The official Marc Bolan web site – http://nataliemcdonald.com/bolan.htm

6.

HOLDING COURT WITH ROBERT FRIPP
THE CRIMSON KING

ONE of the reasons I think Walli and I got along so famously was the fact that both of us were exceedingly interested in UFOs, their minions, and their mission, which all depends upon their individual point of origin.

Walli thought it was possible to established mental contact with the unknown pilots of these craft - many of whom had to be friendly because of their advanced cosmic origins - while I was busy collecting witness testimony, photographs and visiting landing sites where trace markings and impressions had been left in the ground.

I had also become a stringer for a group of national tabloids including the "*Enquirer*." During the period I worked for them they were a legitimate news source. When presenting them with a story I had to provide verifiable backup documents including tapes of the interviews. They were always in need of UFO accounts given by the rich and famous. Walli lined me up with a number of her contacts in the music business.

THE PHILOSOPHY OF ROBERT FRIPP

Of all the musicians who were charmed by Walli you would have to put British guitarist, composer and record producer Robert Fripp at the top of the list. Born 16 May 1946, Fripp has been the only member to have played in all of "King Crimson's" line-ups from their inception in the late 1960s to the present. The band has been known for laying down some really incredibly eerie tracks, such as their primary hits, "*Court of the Crimson King*" and "*Twentieth Century Schizoid Man.*" Fripp has also done an incredible amount of solo work in conjunction with David Bowie, Brian Eno and Darrell Hall of Hall and Oates fame.

Though his onstage appearance was, at least when Walli introduced him to me, that of a "long-haired" rocker, in real life, Robert Fripp it turns

Robert Fripp had planned to produce Walli's spoken word album on witchcraft. He revealed his UFO sighting and went on a skywatch with the author.

out was very down to earth. There is a very "serious" side to him that includes a profound interest in philosophy and things metaphysical. He considered himself a student of philosophers Ouspensky, Ggurdjeff and J.G. Bennett , going so far as to spend ten months in a "continuous education" retreat in Shelbourne to further his studies which included a belief in the life of the soul and its "higher bodies." The belief being that time consists of more than one dimension and at death we continue on in these other linear dimensions." At the time when such topics were broached I think I was still in grade school, though I have recently expanded my own thinking into the realm of coincidences and computer simulations. Interested readers should check out my book, "*The Matrix Control System of Philip K Dick and the Paranormal Synchronicities of Tim Beckley*"

Yes! See how far I have come along in my esoteric studies?

As a side note, one of Robert Fripp's closest allies in the search for spiritual truth seems to have been an unlikely candidate to have been smitten by mysticism and its great masters. Explaining further, one music maven, Monica Surlyage, focusing her attention on the period of the Seventies and one of its key figures Daryl Hall - whom Fripp produced during that era—has this to say in an on line column for "*The Talko*,"

DARYL HALL   **ROBERT FRIPP**

SACRED SONGS

Fripp produced the very creative Daryl Hall. They both shared an interest in the occult.

quoting Daryl extensively:

"Who knew the blonde haired half of Hall & Oates was interested in witchcraft? 'Around 1974, I graduated into the occult, and spent a solid six or seven years immersed in the Kabbala and the Chaldean, Celtic, and Druidic traditions [and] ancient techniques for focusing the inner flame," he said when interviewed by Penthouse in 1987.

"During this time he worked on an album with Robert Fripp of King Crimson called 'Sacred Songs.' A track titled 'Without Tears' is based on the book 'Magick without Tears' by Aleister Crowley. The pop rock singer has also claimed to be related to Crowley and the great-grandson of a male witch. Many of Hall's lyrics allude to his interest in esoteric magick but it seems that recently the singer has cooled off on his occult studies. Hall told Pitchfork, 'A lot of people go through that kind of thing. And I went through it, and I retained a lot of it, and I discarded a lot of it. My life was unbalanced at the time when I was doing that.'"

Hopefully, the study of witchcraft helped with this singer's "balancing act." If Walli were still with us I do believe her philosophical output would have increased and many of those who later adapted other forms of spiritism would still be professing their kinship with Wicca, which has only grown in popularity since the White Witch discovered a belief she could believe in and share.

I can't help but think that Walli might have been a key influence on these individuals, for it was at about this time, a bit before actually, that I first met Fripp backstage at the Academy of Music where we all pretty much congregated. During a lull in the music, I handed Robert a day glow poster of the "Water Bearer" taken from a deck of Tarot cards I had helped to create at the time with Paul Karasic a singer/song writer I was attempting to break into the musical scene.

FRIPP'S BALL OF FIRE

Later Fripp and I got together to exchange ideas and I even went to a wedding with him when a member of his fraternal order of musicians got hitched.

Of course I wanted to know if Robert was into the "UFO scene" or not? I remember him remarking something to the effect that, "It's hard to believe that there isn't life on other planets and that they haven't visited here from time to time," he reminded me in his native British accent which many of the ladies found so charming.

Apparently he did have at least a fleeting (no pun intended) interest in the topic upon being visited by a "stranger" in the night sky. He had parked his van not too far from Stonehenge and was "moving some equipment around in the back" when he happened to look out the rear of the van and saw this "brilliant ball of light go streaking across the starry sky."

"I've always been fascinated with the concept of UFOs and would like to get a good look at one someday," reinforcing his interest in the topic.

Walli lead the sky watch, as Beckley and Fripp hold hands in an attempt to send a telepathic message to the Space Brothers. Photo by Jeffrey Goodman

Sometime later, he joined a group of skywatchers including Walli and myself and was given the opportunity to expand his horizons even more.

THE SKYWATCH

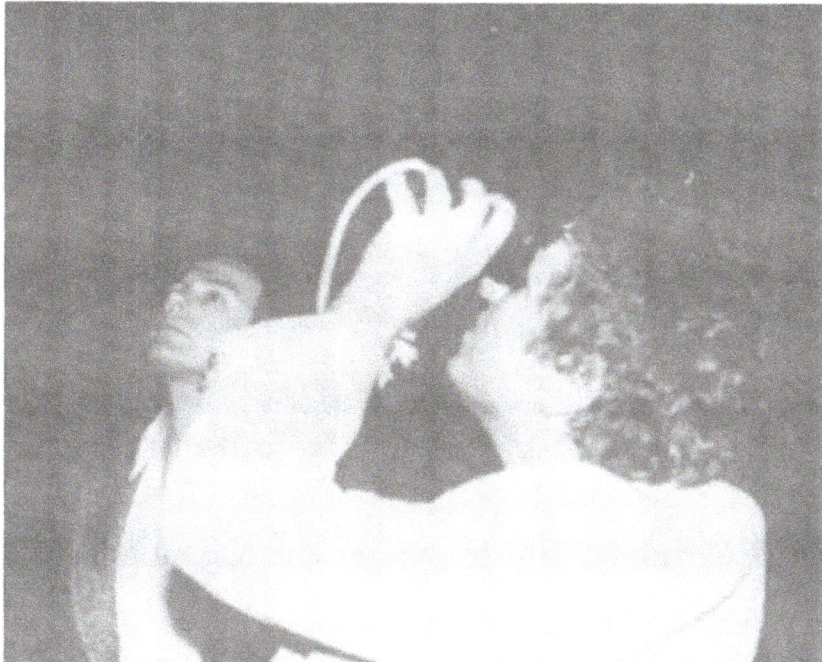

For a moment Fripp and Beckley thought the UFOs might be coming. Courtesy *Manhattan Gazette*, photo by Jeff Goodman.

I could have kicked myself for not keeping a diary of some sort, but it seems to me that Fripp and the White Witch had recently returned from England where they had worked on the never to be released "*Cosmic Children of Love*" album.

As I recall there had been a UFO landing on the other side of the Hudson in Jersey which involved a gentleman seeing several humanoid beings descending down a ramp as a strange disc landed in a park in Bergen County. The occupants scooped up some soil and took off in a flash leaving the witness baffled. There had been other witnesses to the event and the case was written up in the "*Village Voice*," which was a first, as I don't believe the weekly had ever published a UFO story before.

This was a time of other UFO sightings in the New York area, and even John Lennon had seen a brightly lit craft from a perch on his balcony overlooking Central Park and had reported it to the "*New York Daily News*." Muhammad Ali had also observed a heavenly visitor as he was out jogging getting ready for a fight early one morning. Actually, it was two objects like "huge light bulbs" that hung suspended near some apartment buildings on the Upper East Side, the champ told me first hand as we retraced his footsteps at around 4 am, while a few early bird reporters listened in to our conversation with puzzled looks no less.

Walli had always considered herself a highly developed sensitive, and it dawned on her that it might be possible to communicate with the occupants of these craft being seen in her neighborhood in Manhattan and to bring them closer to establish some sort of contact.

Celebrity Ruth Warrick talks to Walli (drink in hand) as a "Daily News" scribe takes mental notes. Courtesy *Manhattan Gazette*. Photo by Jeff Goodman.

We ended up on her roof – she lived in a high-rise just off the park on the Upper East Side – holding hands in a circle sending out the best of vibes and opening ourselves up for a return message from any space people who might be hovering nearby.

Walli lead everyone in a meditation to set the proper mood. Those present included Robert Fripp, Carol Rodriguez and Ruth Warrick who was then starring in the ABC soap opera "*All My Children*." Ruth loved the subject and had turned up at several UFO related events we held during this period. The "*New York Daily News*" even sent over a reporter to cover the contact attempt.

We formed a circle, eyes were closed and a "message" of peace and good will was beamed to the clouds. And while they didn't show themselves as far as we know on this physical level, several of those attending the sky watch did feel the presence of a "higher force," including Walli and Marc Brinkerhoff, a gentleman who says he has been in telepathic contact with the UFOnauts for most of his life and has even photographed them from his apartment window not just blocks away.

"People shouldn't laugh," Walli ended the sky watch. "We should try to keep an open mind, and we might eventually find ourselves in touch with the cosmos. Open contact could happen soon. This I know through psychic means! Walli concluded.

The hunt for UFOs goes on!

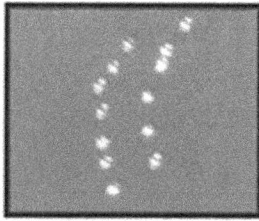

Formation, Upper West Side, from living room window, NYC Nov. 1, 2010

Golden Saturn UFO, Upper West Side, from living room window, NYC June 29, 2011 - movie film.

Morphing orbs with saucer shape UFO shot on Upper West Side, NYC, from living room window, Aug. 14, 2010.

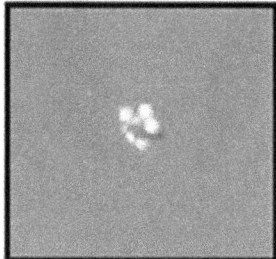

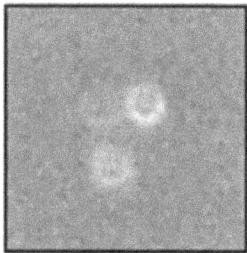

Morphing saucer shapes shot from Cooper Union, NYC, on way to visit my friend, Ingo Swann on my birthday, May 18, 2012.

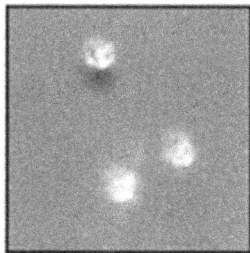

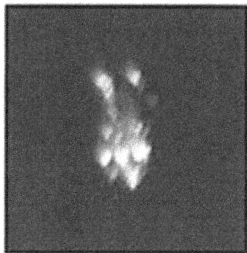

75 Morphing UFO images - Central Park NY April 18, 2015.

Morphing cylinder shape UFO Lexington & 86th bus stop, NYC, May 6, 2012.

MARC BRINKERHOFF
Conscious Channel, Contactee, Author
UFO Photorapher, Mystic Artist

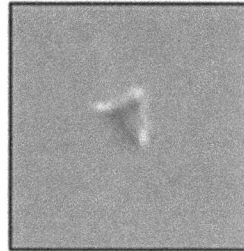

7 morphing UFOs MOMA Sculpture Garden, NYC with 3 witnesses Aug. 23, 2012.

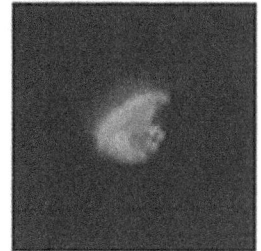

41 morphing UFO images - Central Park NYC May 14, 2015

3 UFOs traveling in formation captured outside my living room window on the Upper West Side of NY, Nov. 13, 2010.

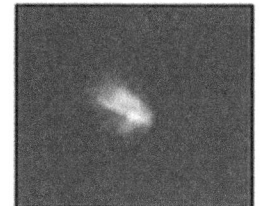

26 morphing UFO images - Central Park NYC Aug. 10, 2015

A few blocks away from Walli's apartment Marc Brinkerhoff sees and photographs UFOs on a regular basis. This is but a small copyrighted©version of his collection.
See book, "*UFO Repeaters - The Camera Doesn't Lie.*"

http://www.MarcBrinkerhoff.com/
http://www.IntergalacticMission.com/

THE TWELVE BOWIES

BOWIE DOESN'T DIE. BOWIE JUST REGENERATES
INTO A NEW BODY WHEN HIS OLD ONE WEARS OUT.
I DON'T KNOW ABOUT YOU, BUT I CALL TIMELORD...

7.

CANDLE MAGICK - CASTING SPELLS

WITCHES believe that you can enhance a spell by burning specific colored candles. It is believed by practicing candle magick that the burning of a candle or candles can go a long way in activating or energizing a spell. There is a world of information available on the use of candles in spell casting. We would suggest any of the books by Maria D'Andrea or William Alexander Oribello, which we happen to publish.

Carol Ann Rodriguez says that Walli taught her how to use candles so that she got positive results almost every time she decided to do a spell.

"I would write my goal, which was a job in a preschool, on a small piece of paper. Then while taking deep regular breaths and concentration and visualizing myself working with children I would write my name around the stated goal (see example).

Student of the craft, Carol Ann says to enhance a money spell write your name in a "circle" over and over and place the amount you are requesting inside.

"As soon as I completed the circle, I would release the thought form by quickly thinking of something else while burning the paper in a green candle."

SIZE AND SHAPE OF THE CANDLES

The size and shape of the candles can also be taken into consideration though they are not that important. "Use the type of candles you feel most comfortable with," Walli always maintained.

Walli believed strongly in the use of different colored candles when casting a spell. Inspirational art © Carol Ann Rodriguez.

The following list of candle types is meant to be an easy reference. Courtesy "*Witchipedia.*"

Dipped Candles are made by dipping a wick into melted wax repeatedly to allow the layers of wax to coat the wick and previous layers of wax until the desired thickness is achieved.

Taper Candles are the most common candles called for in candle magick. They are long and thin and can be put into candle holders or stuck into the ground or into baked goods. Tea Light Candles are handy for mood lighting and for lighting as an honor or offering. They can easily be placed in a dish or on the ground, on any flat surface, really, without the need for a special holder, though appropriate caution needs to be taken.

Votive Candles are small, molded candles with a flat bottom that can be placed on any surface. They are generally used either for mood lighting or as votive offerings or remembrance candles and are often classified according to the length of time they are expected to burn. These may be called for in spells that last a specific length of time for this reason.

Carol Ann says she got her job by writing out her request and placing it in the flame of a green candle.

Pillar Candles are molded candles with a wide base. They can be quite tall or squat and sometimes have multiple wicks. A triple-wicked pillar candle is popular for honoring the Goddess. The outer surface of the pillar candle can be adorned with pictures, flowers and herbs to further enhance and refine your spellwork.

Jar Candles are created by placing a wick in the center of a jar and filling it with wax. This gives you a candle with its own holder and added safety feature. It can't be dressed the way a taper or pillar candle can be dressed, but the outer surface of the glass jar that contains it can be decorated to suit the occasion. These are often decorated with photographs of people or Saints and burned to honor or propitiate them. Many spellworkers will make their own jar spell candles, combining the spell ingredients with the melted wax before they pour it into the jar.

Figure Candles molded in the shape of a male or female are very potent for those doing a love spell, but hey no cheating and burning one of each gender - unless you're looking to get into some kinky sex magick!

Keep it as simple as you like or as ritualistic as you feel comfortable with. "Your heart should be your judge as to how you wish to progress along the Wiccan path." This would ultimately be the way that Walli would approach this matter.

While the meaning of the different color candles may vary slightly with each practitioner. Carol says Walli taught her what the following colors represented when utilizing them in a ritual or spell.

Oh and there can be some overlapping.

THE COLORS AND THEIR MEANING

GREEN - Money. Prosperity. Career Goals. Success.

YELLOW - Health.

RED - Love. Sexual Desire. Passion. Attraction Of A Soul Mate.

PINK - Pure spiritual love (Not sex..."Though that can be nice too," as Walli used to say.)

ORANGE – Love and lust.

BLUE - Protection. Use freely! ("Walli always burned one during every spell, just to be on the safe side so as not to draw in any negativity," Carol notes).

SILVER - For bringing down the Moon Goddess.

GOLD - For bringing down the Sun God.

Note: Walli never used purple candles.

A FEW WICCAN TYPE SPELLS

If Walli had left a Book of Shadows we could have found the following spells within its handwritten pages. Carol Ann assisted in adapting them to our Wiccan work.

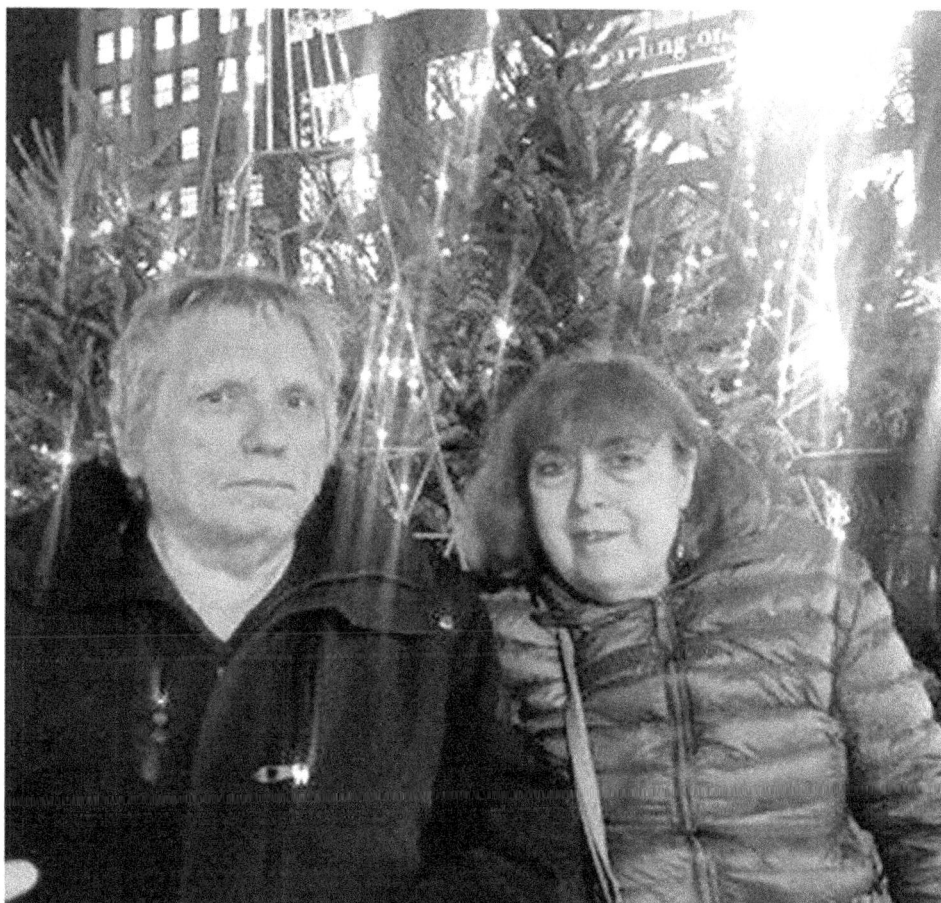

Carol Ann came to the occult center in 1971 for a lecture by Walli Elmlark, and has done art and worked for publisher Tim Beckley oh so many years! -- Photo by April Troiani, with assistance from Big Earl.

SPELL # 1

COURTING A NEW LOVE OR REKINDLING AN OLD ONE

Get out your preferred colored candles (see above list) during the period of a New or Waxing Moon.

Fill a small to medium size glass bowl three quarters of the way to the top with water and add rose petals (suggested red or pink) so that they are floating on the top of the glass.

Obtain a few small white flowers such as "Queen Anne's Lace" and float them around the rose petals.

Place a small twig of rosemary on top of the roses - just a pinch so that it doesn't weigh the petals down.

You should collect an item that reminds you of the person you are trying to attract and also place it on the roses. Maybe a follicle of their hair. It been suggested that if you are looking for a light hearted romance to sprinkle some glitter into the bowl. Walli would have liked that - she loved glitter.

When you have completed your easy to do spell place the bowl onto your windowsill overnight and keep it there for a few days if you like.

The final step is to dump out the water and place the "left over" contents in a little bag which those practicing magick often refer to as a Mojo bag.

SPELL # 2

TO PROTECT AN OBJECT

On your altar (any quiet, out of the way, place where no one will disturb you) place and light a blue candle and a white candle.

Then trace a pentagram over the object you wish to protect and say: with this pentagram protection I lay to guard this object both night and day.

As I say it so, mote it be.

Blessed Be.

SPELL # 3

A SPELL TO OBTAIN MONEY

During the waxing moon, burn a blue and green candle anointed with a money drawing oil.

Write on a small piece of paper the amount of money you need, and place it under the green candle.

Say: "Money, money come to me; this is what I need." Then write your name on the piece of paper completely around the amount. Quickly let the thought form go by burning the paper in the green candle and thinking of something else.

Well there you go. Isn't it easier to become a witch than you might have originally thought? Try a few of "Walli's Spells" and see how they work for you.

Please Note: If you can't find them locally we get all our magickal supplies from:

Azure Green /Abyss Distribution

16 Bell Rd, PO Box 48, Middlefield, MA 01243-0048

Phone: 1-413-623-2155 - www.abyssdistribution.com

Tim and Carol seated at the beginning of a session of the NY School of Occult Arts and Sciences. Time flies faster than a witch's broom.

Walli's spells were sought after by rock stars and celebrities. Popular New Orleans musician Dr. John The Night Tripper who used a bit of gris gris glitter on the audience came to the Occult Center to trade secrets and perform magick on our photographer.
© From The Helen Hovey Collection.

8.

THE CURSE ON ROCK AND ROLL

I don't know who would have placed a full blown curse on rock and roll. But there are too many well respected entertainers who have needlessly died before their time, even with drugs and booze being so prevalent. Perhaps it was some Southern Baptist minister. (My dad was a Southern Baptist so please no flaming). Or maybe it was someone from the temperance movement who thought that every teen listening to Little Richard's "*Good Golly Miss Molly*" (*Sure Like To Ball*) in the back seat of their Chevy, were getting shit faced and making out? Or most probably a group of strict parents living in a small podunk town where rock music and dancing have been banned, just like in the movie "*Footloose.*" In the end your guess is as good as mine or Walli's.

Back in the days of classic rock and roll, New York's White Witch, and I co-authored a book "*Rock Raps of the Seventies,*" which was half text, half pictorial. This large format paperback was filled with interviews, breezy reviews and pictures of some of the greatest rock stars of that era. We had a chapter that caused quite a bit of controversy and some negative mail from fans and even got us a condemnation in "*Crawdaddy,*" a highly respected journal which took the music scene most seriously, perhaps more so than it deserved.

JINX OF THE J - THE 27 CLUB - AND A NY DOLL

Some people seem to be able to predict their own passing. I don't know if it's a gut reaction to some inner feeling, but normally these predictions are foretold well in advance of an individual's transition. The most famous foretelling of someone's own death would be Mark Twain who was born in 1835 on the day that Halley's Comet appeared for the first time in its cycle around the universe. In 1909 as the "avenging rock" was ready to rush past earth the satirist proclaimed that he would be going out with the same comet. He did! Tough ball of ice. Too cold for me to ride on.

But what about individuals in other walks of life? Are there any synchronicities that we can apply that would make it seem their deaths were preordained?

In "*Rock Raps*" there was a chapter "Jinx of the J" which described the unwelcome deaths of numerous famed rocks stars who had a J prominently displayed in their name. There was Janis Joplin, Jim Morrison, John Lennon, Jimi Hendrix, and Brian Jones. Skeptics point out that drugs played a major role in the passing of these musicians, and we don't need to deny that, but so what – that's not part of our equation.

Then we have a much longer list of of rockers who have been inducted into the "27 Club," meaning that they died at the age of 27. Talk about an uninvited calling. A lot of the musicians on the list I don't even recognize like Rudy Lewis (Drifters, vocalist), Peter Ham (Badfinger, keyboardist), Gary Thain (bassist, Uriah Heap), Leslie Harvey (guitar player, Stone The Crows). If you wish to do more research on this by all means do a web search for "27 Club."

Amy Winehouse   Brian Jones   Jimi Hendrix   Janis Joplin

Jim Morrison   Kurt Cobain   Robert Johnson   Jean-Michel Basquiat

Members of the 27 Club, a group you will do anything to stay out of!

A big fan of glam rock, Hell I am even on Edgar Winter's 'Frankenstein' album, notes Tim. Beckley and Walli cohort Ken Currier promoted the First International Glitter Ball at the Hotel Diplomat off Times Square.

Now where these puzzling deaths hit me personally and pretty hard is with the passing of a personal friend. Arthur "Killer" Kane was the bass player for the NYC glam rock band the New York Dolls, who were part of the underground Max's Kansas City crowd lead by Lou Reed's Velvet Underground in the Sixties and Seventies. They predated even David Bowie in strutting around the stage in their six inch platform shoes, mascara, lipstick, and tight fitting silver lemay tops and spandex pants. I had seen the Dolls perform many times. I was hanging out and trying to book some of the other local acts like the Magic Tramps, the Harlots of 42nd Street, and Satan the Eternal Fire Eater. The Dolls were the most popular of the lot, but I would not call them mega stars when compared to Led Zep lets say. They attracted, for the most part an enthusiastic, but not an astronomical following. The record companies were still not into glitter or glam rock (Bowie and Marc Bolan had not made it in the U.S. yet), and the Dolls were being passed over at that point. Which was a shame caused I loved these very theatrical, post punk bands. I was even known as "Mr Glitter," and tried to be as flashy as I could without going to the extreme. Ken Currier, one of Walli's friends (to be introduced more appropriately later on) and I even promoted the First International Glitter Ball at the Hotel Diplomat in Times Square, one of the venues Kiss used to book before they became famous and rich.

Arthur Kane, the bassist for the Dolls and his wife Barbara, and I, became friends. The couple would come to my UFO shows when I held them out west. Those wishing to know more about the UFO experience of Arthur and Barbara Kane should check out an interview I did recently with Barbara which is posted on my YouTube channel, "*Mr UFOs Secret Files*." The rocking couple were both into the subject and once they were even in the audience when I sang at one of the conferences a version of "A-L-I-E-N" to the tune of Hendrix's "Gloria," changing a few of the key words for theatrical effect, and beside it was a UFO event. The "He" being referred to here is of course an alien. The UFO band backed me up, Sue Gordon, Randy Winters, Bleu Ocean, Jerry Wills.

He came into my house

He came up my stairs

He tells me he needs me

He says that he cares

He makes me feel good

He makes me feel good all night

And while this annotate may be past Walli's watch, it's still worth relating as it very much relates to rock and roll. At this point in the late 1980s - early 1990s, the Dolls had broken up years before and Arthur was trying to get a fresh foothold in the ever changing music business. He was finding it difficult and had been overwhelmed by a number of personal problems. It did not look like the band was ever going to get together again. David Johansen, the Doll's lead singer was the only one really forging a career as an actor ("*Car 54 Where Are You?*") and a solo artist (Buster Poindexter).

Then, in 2004, the influential frontman Morrisey from the Smiths put together a reunion tour for the Dolls getting the surviving members back together again. Soon after I got a call from Arthur who seemed exceedingly happy as he had felt the world had passed him by and now he was back in the mix (musical mix that is) once again. The band was in rehearsal at the time in the UK, but they would soon be coming to America. They would be playing at an outdoor concert on Randall's Island Park in the middle of the

East River and Arthur was putting me on the back stage guest list.

As the date approached for the show, I tried to get in touch with Arthur on several occasions to see if there were any special instructions like what day and what time should I show up and at what back stage entrance to go to in order to pick up my pass. I never heard from Arthur again. I got a call from my drummer friend Bleu Ocean that Arthur had died.

Turns out he died on my birthday July 13th 2004, so now I think of him every year around this time and pay my regards to Barbara Kane who used to bring their beautiful, pure breed, white wolf to my conference. I never saw her shape shift but we once did fight over a bowl of potato chips when she scooped the last couple of chips out with her long tongue. I let her take them. She was my guest after all. Found out later "Killer" Kane had thought he had a bad case of the flu while in London and upon arriving in the States checked himself into a Los Angeles hospital complaining of fatigue. He was quickly diagnosed with leukemia and died within two hours at the age of fifty five. David Johansen described Kane as "nonjudgmental, bawdy and holy."

If you're interested in the glitter scene and in Arthur Kane's career there is a streaming video version or a DVD titled, "*New York Doll*." In the last few years before his passing, Arthur became a devout member of the Church of Jesus Christ of Latter-day Saints; once again a strong God connection is implied. He is missed. And another death dealing synchronicity in my life is hopefully put to rest for good.

By the way for those of you who are students of classical music check out what is known as the Curse of the Ninth which, in essence, is the urban legend that says that a ninth symphony is destined to be a composer's last, and will die after writing it, or completing a tenth. I never knew Mozart or Beethoven so there is no six degrees of separation here or anything to apply possible coincidences involving their deaths.

This wasn't the type of music Walli nor I were into, so thank God we're leaving the "Twilight Zone" behind; though we are a short ways away from entering the arena of "*The Exorcist*," with the possession of a famous celebrity Walli became involved with. In the meanwhile, Walli and I have other chilling tales to tell.

Holding a copy of "*UFO Universe*," which author Tim Beckley edited for a dozen years, NY Dolls bass player Arthur Kane passed away on Tim's birthday after they had planned to meet backstage at an outdoor festival.

9.
JIMI HENDRIX- SPACE IS THE PLACE

WALLI used to talk about him all the time.

Jimi Hendrix was a star seedling if there ever was one.

"He's been reincarnated on earth to help raise the vibrations of the planet. His job is to instruct the young people, even though he may not fully realize what his mission is.

Photo © The Helen Hovey Collection

Walli believed strongly that Hendrix had a mission as a "cosmic educator," but his mission was short lived.

"A lot of these starchildren," Walli explained, "get mixed up with drugs and alcohol. These are the emissaries among us. Some know who they are. Others do not! But they realize they are quite different from the average person. They may even be misfits in the physical world.

"UFOs have been known to follow Jimi around," Walli told me, and eventually I found this to be true.

I can't say in all honesty that I really knew Jimi Hendrix, but I did see him give a number of really good performances in a couple of intimate, clubs in Greenwich Village. This was long before he flew off to England and came back on his way to be a star.

It was at one of those post-Woodstock concerts where I managed to wind my way backstage, and I admit I was pretty high myself. Jimi Hendrix was leaning up against a wall of amps and speakers. As I walked past him, we both just kind of nodded as if we recognized each other, and to this day I can swear I heard him ask me, "And what planet are you from pal?" I would say that was damn perceptive of him since he didn't know me from an alien in a wormhole.

Oh and hey, I never took acid again. No need to. I figured I had been to the "top of the mountain," watching the musical notes drift out of Jimi's speakers in living color, - just like a real "purple haze."

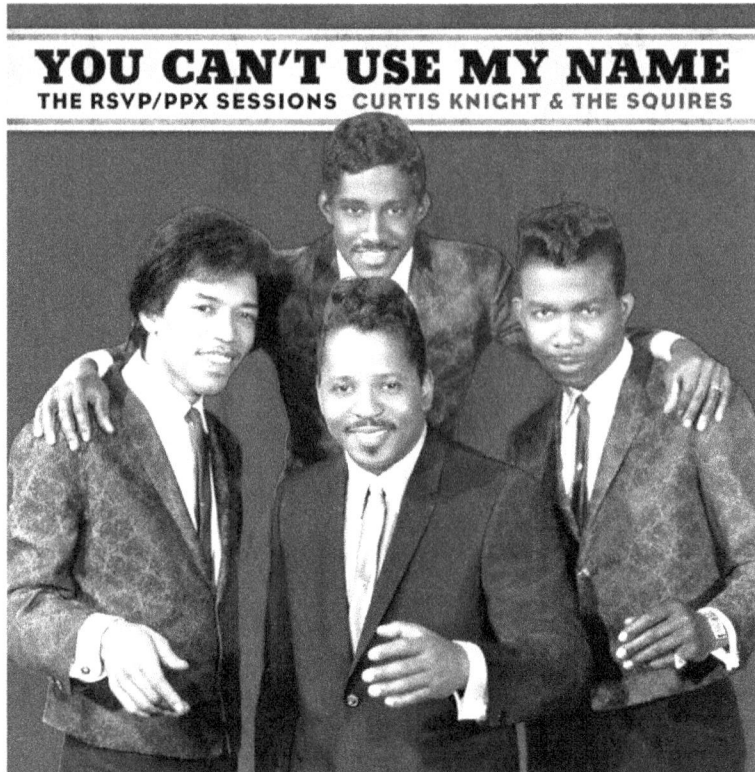

Hendrix and Curtis (center front) were in the pre-Hendrix Experience band known as the "Squires."

David Henderson, in his book "*The Life of Jimi Hendrix*" (Bantam), quotes Jimi's feelings about life on other planets: "There are other people in the solar system, you know, and they have the same feelings too, not necessarily bad feelings, but see, it upsets their way of living for instance - and they are a whole lot heavier than we are . . . But like the solar system is going through a change soon and it's going to affect the Earth in about 30 years." I can just imagine him smoking weed as he went on and on in his pronouncements.

On several occasions during his career, UFOs just happened to show up while Jimi was in the middle of a concert. During the last days of his life, he performed on the rim of an extinct volcano in Maui. Jimi played three 45-minute sets, and after each set, he retired to a special sacred Hopi Indian tent. Later, witnesses in Maui testified that they heard musical tones emanating from rocks and stones. UFOs were also sighted over the volcano by people who called in to a local radio show. A cameraman on the set said that he fell from his perch after seeing a UFO through his lens.

UFOS AND THE RAINBOW BRIDGE CONTACT

In the doc movie "*Rainbow Bridge*," filmed at an occult center on Maui, Hendrix rattles on for several minutes about astral projection and the philosophy of the Space Brothers, who are even referenced to as Aryan-type humanoids. Jimi also talks about mastering the art of psychic healing through the use of color and sound. Fellow musician, songwriter and bass player, Curtis Knight, who had performed in "The Squires" with Hendrix knew all about the episode involving the UFO in Maui. "It was," he said, "an odd-looking craft that glittered in the bright sunlight."

As print time rolled around I came across an edition of the glossy "*Mauitime*" in which there was a lengthy review by Anuhea Yagi on the making of "*Rainbow Bridge*." The magazine went back and interviewed some of those involved in the making of the movie which had limited distribution, not being a purely concert film, but a sounding board for hippies to talk about the coming of a predicted New Age of enlightenment.

"Chuck Wein (Director) wanted to produce a program to relieve mass paranoia against the arrival of extraterrestrials," says Potts. "[He] was talking about UFOs because he believed that evil power monopolies ran the planet, along with the military industrial complex, and UFOs were powered by electromagnetic energy. If this were to come out, it'd be a bigger revolution than the Industrial Revolution, because electromagnetic energy would replace oil electricity. We went into a lot of detail about that, but most of it was not in the film."

Note, that Hawaii has always been a hot spot for UFO activity though most mainlanders are ignorant of the fact. Hawaii is steeped in all sorts of supernatural legends and lore. If you have a moment, catch my appearance on "*Mysteries of the National Parks*." Season One, Episode Six, "*Firestarter*." YouTube: www.youtube.com/watch?v=moFntsZdz9U

Jimi felt certain the UFO had come down to put its spiritual stamp of approval on the show. He told Curtis Knight that he had been emotionally and physically recharged by the experience. During the course of our conversation, Curtis also revealed the fascinating details of the time a UFO landed in front of them and actually saved their lives. The event took place on a cold winter's night near Woodstock, NY in 1965.

In a cover story the glossy *"Mauitime"* goes back a bit to the making of *"Rainbow Bridge"* starring Jimi Hendrix.

A UFO SAVED JIMI'S LIFE!

According to Curtis, if it hadn't been for the occupants of this metallic stranger, Jimi and his fellow musicians might have frozen to death. "It was four o'clock in the morning, and we were trying to make it back to Manhattan - a drive of more than 100 miles – through the worst blizzard I can recall. The wind was whipping the snow around our van so fiercely that we missed the turn-off leading to the state highway that would put us in the direction of home. The next thing I remember is getting stuck in a drift that reached the hood of our vehicle. Soon it got so cold. The windows were rolled up tight, and we had the heater on full blast to protect us from the rawness of the elements. I had my doubts about seeing the light of day. We could have turned to human icicles very easily. That's how bitter it was!"

Curtis says the road in front of them suddenly lit up, as a bright phosphorescent cone-shaped object, like a space capsule landed in the snow about 100 feet up ahead. It stood on tripod landing gear, and for all purposes gave the appearance of being something right out of science fiction. At first we thought it was an apparition caused by the cold and our confused state of mind. I mean, we just couldn't believe our eyes."

Prodding Jimi with his elbow, Curtis asked if his imagination was playing tricks on him or whether the rock star saw it too. Jimi didn't answer, but sort of smiled. He seemed to be staring out into the night, his eyes riveted on this thing resting within a stone's throw. Curtis was overcome with fright. Before he could make a move of any kind, a door opened on the side of the craft and an entity came forth. He stood eight foot tall, his skin was yellowish, and instead of eyes, the creature had slits. His forehead came to a point, and his head ran straight into his chest, leaving the impression that he had no neck.

The being proceeded to float to the ground and glide towards the trapped occupants of the van. It was then that Curtis noticed the snow was melting in the wake of the creature. His body generated tremendous heat, so much so that as it came across a small rise, the snow disappeared around in all directions.

"In a matter of what seemed like seconds, the being came over to the right-hand side of the van where Jimi was seated and looked right through the window. Jimi seemed to be communicating telepathically with it."

Curtis relates that immediately the interior of their vehicle began to heat up.

"Suddenly, I was roasting! One moment it had been bitter cold, and the next moment we might as well have been in Haiti."

The heat coming from the being evaporated the snow was enough, says Curtis, to free their imprisoned van.

"As it glided behind our van, I saw the drift had completely vanished. Turning on the ignition key, I gunned the motor and got out of there. As I looked back through the rear view window, I could see the road filling in with snow again. The object – the strange craft – was at the same instant lifting off like a rocket from a launching pad. Jimi never did talk much about what happened. He sort of let me know that the cool thing to do was not to bring up the subject. It was to be our little secret.

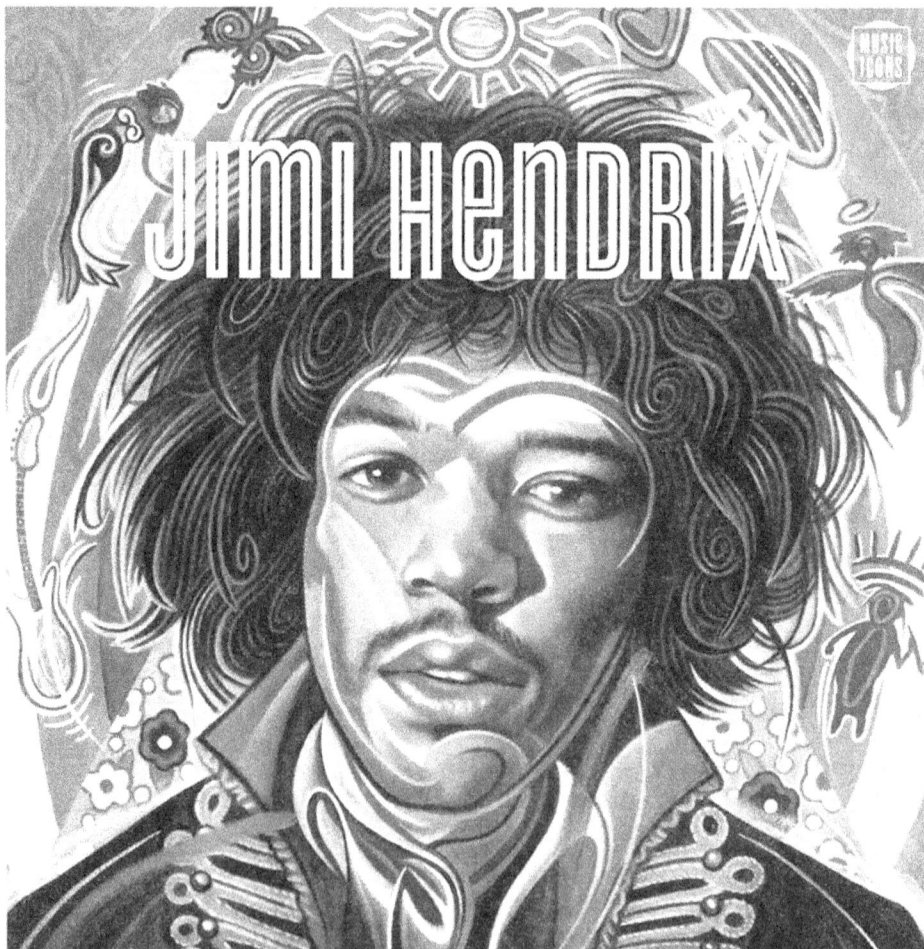

With a UFO hovering over his afro (right side) the USPS honored Hendrix with this commemorative stamp.

"However, from what he did say, I sort of suspect that the object arrived to save our necks chiefly because Jimi had been practicing trying to communicate by ESP with the beings on board. I know this may be hard to believe, but I'm putting it straight, just like it happened, you hear?

"The boys from the group who were with us remember nothing. They were out cold in the back. As we got into the main road, they revived. It is as if they had been placed under a spell – you know – hypnotized."

A capsule review of Jimi's songs shows that he incorporated some of his interplanetary ties in with his music. The lyrics of many of his songs contain veiled references to UFOs. His album, *"Axis: Bold as Love,"* opens with an announcer talking about flying saucers, with a cut following being a catchy tune called, *"Up From the Stars."*

Though Jimi and Walli and Curtis have all passed from the earth plane, it wouldn't be hard to imagine that somewhere out there, they are looking down over the earth and smiling. We certainly do miss the vibrant star child, the White Witch and the gossiping song writer/bass player who were once in our midst and on a UFO binge.

All Along the Watch Tower... the UFO watch tower.

"Elemental" Original Art ©CAROL ANN RODRIGUEZ.

10.

THE MAGICKAL WIZARDRY OF VAUGHN BODĒ

Vaughn and his creation Cheech Wizard had one thing in common - the love of top hats.

THE bushy haired artist had moved in with Walli.

There was some talk that they were going to join forces and hit the road together combining the occult with art, perhaps as an extension of a Cartoon Concert Tour that had already been formulated and underway. Was it possible to attract a sophisticated audience into both witchcraft and underground adult comics? Certainly this would prove to be a hybrid of genres if it worked out as envisioned.

Such a "burnt offering" to the gods had never been tried before, but the occult was catching on with teenagers and college students and here you had a couple whose image could easily be marketed with the right promotion to a large, potential, audience. In fact, in addition to Walli's lecturing at my occult center she had hooked up with the American Program Bureau out of Boston and was doing talks at various colleges around the country. She was finally getting paid for her endeavors and that was a plus when considering that most, if not all, of her spells she did for free.

Vaughn Bodē's unique talents were already being recognized by an aggressive management company touring him in a show "*The Cartoon Concert*" that featured the artist vocalizing his characters, while their depictions were projected on a silver screen behind him.

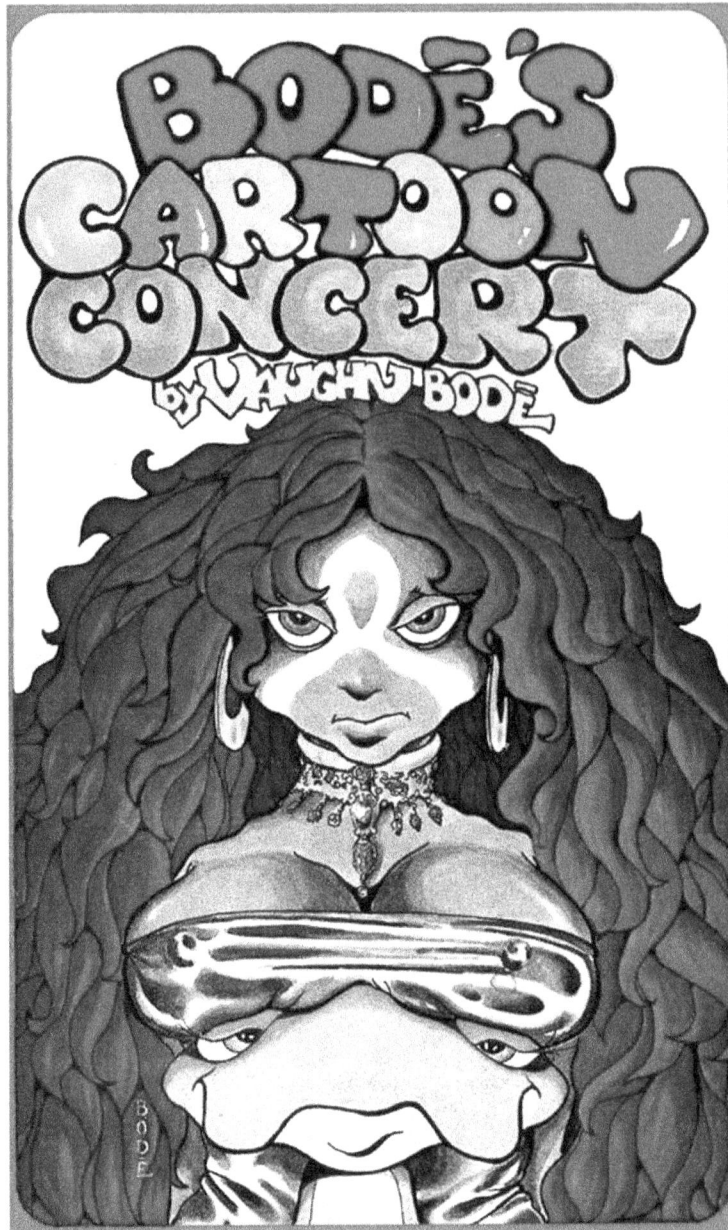

It was planned for Walli to join the tour.

The young underground cartoonist, born in Utica, NY, 1941, had managed to attract a hip—largely male—audience with his full busted ladies and contemporary adult orientated illustrations. His work appeared in various avant garde "men's sophisticates" (a classier term for soft core porn magazines like "*Swank*" and "*Cavalier*"), with his main character Cheech Wizard taking on a life of his own and winning him the prestigious Hugo Award. Cheech and his creator wore a high hat and I often thought this might have influenced Marc Bolan chapeau choice.

By no means did Vaughn shy away from controversy as his personal foray into the world of erotica and mysticism was pretty well established as noted by a Zagria.blogspot.com scribe:

"He pioneered putting sexual content in comics and cartoons, and inspired others. He was a heterosexual swinger, participating in group sex. He boasted how he had had sex with four women in four different cities in four days. . . By 1970 his interest in transvestism had developed from looking at pictures to dressing in private. As he continued to desire women, he believed that he must be a unique 'unisexual', a forerunner of humans to come. He started wearing female slacks, blouses and boots, grew his nails long, and began carrying a shoulder bag."

In 1971 in New York he met Guru Maharaj Ji, and felt that he had received his holiness. He chose to attain full enlightenment by the fast track of using autoerotic asphyxiation to induce mystical experiences. This sexual fetish – spiritual or not – lead to his untimely death.

THE WIZARD'S PASSING

It's no secret how Vaughn succumbed. He was searching for the light and ended up accidentally hanging himself with a strap. In fact, when I met Vaughn's son Mark under the strangest of circumstances he outright asked me if I knew what had happened to his dad. I confirmed that I did because Walli had gone over the details with me, mentioning that it was Mark who had found Bodē's lifeless form.

The following is a recap of that day as told by Bob Levin in a lengthy article in "*Fantagraphics, A Comic Journal.*"

"At approximately 1:00 p.m., on Friday, July 18, 1975, the cartoonist Vaughn Bodē came out of the bedroom of

The Wizard stands guard at door to his castle.

VAUGHN BODĒ DEAD AT 33

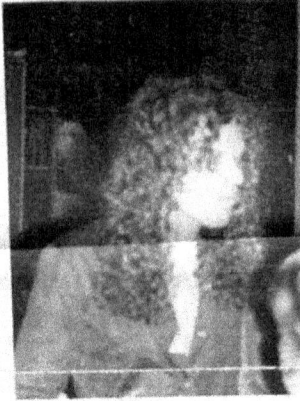

Just literally minutes before press time on this issue we were informed of the death of VAUGHN BODE. Reports say Mr. Bodē was involved in yoga and was suspended from the ceiling in an affair involving ropes when he came out of a trance and started getting undone. Something apparently slipped, and he was accidentally hung. The accident occurred on Friday, July 18. Berni Wrightson, close friend of Bodē's, stresses the point that it was definitely an accident. His death, especially at such a young age, is very, very sad.

Watered down death notice for the fans posted at comic con.
booksteveslibrary.blogspot.com/2006/07/vaughn-bode.html

the apartment in San Francisco's Mission District he shared with a lover (I will call Helene) who worked as a secretary at UC Medical Center. He wore a monk's robe and several necklaces. His light brown hair hung in curls to his shoulders. His blue eyes were lined and mascaraed. A white triangle was painted on his forehead.

"No phone calls today, Mark," he said to his 12-year-old son, visiting from New York. "I'm doing my God thing."

"You look beautiful," Mark said. His father smiled.

"You see, Mark, I really am a high priest."

Can't help but wonder if Walli had initiated him, a question we shall never have answered.

"He returned to his room," continues Levin. "In the center, on the lid of a coffin, sat a Buddha, a Jesus, a Krishna; figures in the pantheon of a religion he was creating. Over the next few hours, to the accompaniment of Mozart and pausing only to slip $5.00 under the door for Mark to buy food, he worked through a series of steps as ritualized as a Japanese tea ceremony. He believed that each human sense was a window through which God communicated. This communication could be magnified by alternately silencing each sense. So he applied blindfold, earplugs, gloves, apparatuses to mute taste and smell, each increasing his expectations and excitements as he approached a climactic extinguishing of his conscious self."

ONLY IN THE MOVIES

Walli always used to say that there were no coincidences...that nothing happened by chance. "There is a reason for everything," she reiterated. She would have really grooved on all the synchronicities that have been piling up in my life, most of which have transpired since W.E. "went away." And we're not talking about thinking of someone and you run into them in the street a day or two later, or you wake up and it says 4:44 on the alarm clock (never could see the significance in that "coincidence," best time to hit the can maybe?).

Now I'm talking about real zingers as related in the following incident which involved both father and son. My own research on synchronicities (see my book "*The Matrix of Philip K. Dick and the Paranormal Synchronizations of Timothy Green Beckley*") shows that there is a huge tie in with matters involving the deceased and these outrageous synchronizations. I would believe that Walli's spirit hand might have played a role in this epic incident in my hook up with unexplainable phenomena. This is the type of stuff Walli spoke of at the New York School of Occult Arts and Science.

* * * * * *

She was absolutely striking. Very attractive. "Hot." I knew she would look sexy behind the camera and I was certainly looking for a sexy actress to star in an upcoming horror movie I was planning to shoot in about a month.

I had placed an ad in "*Backstage*," looking for undiscovered talent, which is code for we are not union and can't afford to pay very much. Received lots of calls from gals who wanted to hear more about what we were doing. "Shooting a vampire movie," I explained to those who responded. And you know lady vampires have to be seductive. It's part of what draws an audience. There was, I went on, some nudity, but nothing outrageous, as I was going for an R rating. Four or five gals showed up. I was not overwhelmed until this one starlet-in-waiting appeared and abruptly took my breath away.

Dark hair. Slender. Thin waste. Perky in all the right anatomical places. I would have hired her on the spot, but I wasn't running a casting couch. I actually interviewed those wanting to be in the movie. I knew most didn't have much, if any, experience, but you want your Scream Queens to be, outside of pretty, talented enough to deliver a line and shriek on cue. I had each of the actresses scream for two or three minutes in front of the camera, pull their hair and generally act like they were being attacked by some maniac. The screams were so piercing that I was certain someone in the building was going to call the cops, thinking that an actual murder was taking place.

Teresa did everything well enough to offer her a starring role, which she accepted without hesitation. We were both hoping this would be the start of a nice career in the performing arts for her, despite the film's low budget. You can find "*Barely Legal Lesbian Vampires*," somewhere on YouTube and you won't even have to pay to watch it. My treat.

As we sat chatting on the couch, I had an open notebook to scribble down whatever I needed to remember. There were a couple of pens in front of us and I noticed that Teresa was doodling in a sketch pad. It looked like a cross between graffiti art and some sort of cartoon character, but I was at a bad angle to get a very good look or otherwise I might have recognized the figure she was sketching.

Curiosity getting the better of me, I asked her what she was drawing. "Oh, it's an artist whose work I think is super cool." It was like she was channeling; she was so busy working on her doodle that I began to think she was deliberately ignoring our conversation. "There is this underground cartoonist," she explained. "He's deceased now. His name is Vaughn Bodē, and his principal character that everyone loves so much is called Cheech Wizard."

Turns out, the Wizard was once described, "as a pot-smoking, pot-inspired, hedonistic mystic with an earthy libido for voluptuous babes. It was a funny and sexy cartoon," wrote critic Mark Emery.

Boy was I floored!

I had met Vaughn years before through Walli while he was staying at her place. The meeting remained in my mind because he was such a nonconformist that he stood out in a crowd – even in our crowd.

Remarks cartoon archivist Craig Yow, "Vaughn stood out even in that hippie era and in New York, where you expect the unconventional. Vaughn Bodē looked like Jesus. Long white robe and hair like Jesus wore it. Hallelujah, I adored it! The robe and the hair were joined by long fingernails - bright blue in color."

In fact, sorry I don't believe I've mentioned it until now, but **Bodē** had once done a cartoon panel of Walli in the same style as Cheech, but, then again, they certainly were both wizards.

Teresa was duly impressed that I knew who her favorite artist was. And I guess she should have been, as Bodē was not exactly in the same league as Peter Max, though they were contemporaries. Bodē's work was for a select clientele, a slightly more hip audience, as it was full of voluptuous women, just like Teresa and one over-the-top male wizard who was always in search of a party.

She was even more surprised that I had met her favorite artist, but our reflections on the cartoonist ended at that point, until it was bought up several months later through an unexpected turn of events.

One Friday or Saturday, they were showing independent, low budget movies in the back room of Max Fish's on Orchard Street in Greenwich Village. The bar's Facebook page describes the place as "a legendary LES NYC bar/Art Gallery/Skater, Musician and Oddball Haunt opened in 1989." You will have to figure out what Skater (a form of music?) and LES (lesbian?) stand for, but I didn't see any of that in the back room where a projector was throwing a tiny micro-budget flick on the wall.

Eventually Teresa and I adjourned to a table near the bar for a drink. The place was fairly crowded and everyone was in a good mood, chatting among themselves and making new friends as one is apt to do in a Les/Skater watering hole in the Village. One young fellow took a seat across from us, and we engaged him in conversation. Somehow the subject of art came up, something I know little about, and which doesn't interest me.

The young man said his father had been a relatively well-known artist and he was following in his dad's footsteps. His name was – hold onto your garter belts, ladies, and your suspenders, gentlemen   Mark Bodē! Apparently, Mark was in town, I think from Boston, to arrange the sale of some art, whether his or Vaughn's, I don't remember. From what I gather, Mark often produces works similar to the elder Bodē's style and is best known for his works "*Cobalt-60*," "*Miami Mice*" and "*The Lizard of Oz.*"

Naturally, I told him I had met his dad, but he was skeptical until I said we were both mutual friends of the White Witch of New York Walli Elmlark. "That's a name I haven't heard for a long, long time," Mark admitted. We chatted for a while and eventually said our goodbyes, though we had a more than passing synchronicity under our belts to refer to. I mean, Teresa, my stunning new actress, had been doodling in the style of the late artist the first night I met her, and here we run into his son out of the blue. I had never been to this bar before in my life (in this reality anyway). I don't think Mark had, not sure about Teresa.

So go figure, and have a good time at Max Fish's while you're doing it.

Truly Bodē – as had Walli – had created his own world of fantasy to make up for a disastrous childhood at the hands of abusive parents. Bodē's life unfortunately came to an untimely and premature end by his own hand, while experimenting with erotic asphyxiation He died, in July 1975, "coincidentally" at the age of 37, the same age that some believe Jesus had also died. Once again, Jesus becomes part of the synchronized equation, as if he too were created by those cloaked figures behind the Matrix.

A blast from the past - "early" Walli Elmlark.
Photo from the Michael Lawrence Collection.

TROUBLED TIMES AND FAMILY VALUES

Tim and Natalie - Naz - Kosubal still crazy after all these years.

Carol Ann says she felt bad when Vaughn and Walli went their separate way. They were just not feeling the vibe. I think Walli found Bodē's sexuality to be "further along," than anything she might see as being part of sexual magick and her Wiccan beliefs, which were certainly not straight or conservative by any means.

Walli, and we won't dwell on this, also "ended it all" when she took an overdose of barbiturates around 1980. Carol Ann says news reached Elmlark's friends through a member of Walli's family. It was stunning news and hard to believe. "I always thought it was suspicious that we hadn't gotten word of this in any other way nor did we see any notice in the papers. I wondered if perhaps they had her whisked away and maybe committed. My spirit guides would not confirm what we had been told."

I know this sounds like a wild conspiracy theory, but you can never rule anything out.

"Walli's parents never approved of her life style or her belief in witchcraft," my long time friend Natalie Kosubal reminded me. I met the dazzling young "Naz" backstage at the Academy of Music while she was hanging out with members of the colorful band *"Teenage Lust."* She was pretty close to Walli, had been to her apartment on plenty of occasions, and had spoken intimately with her. "Every time Walli went to see her folks she came back to her place really depressed. It was like they wanted to drive a stake through her heart." There are those who believe that her continued confrontation with her mom and dad drove her to take more and more drugs which had been prescribed by her doctors. There were those in the occult community who were also putting the whamy on her because their beliefs and practices – black magick? – were different than hers."

"Walli's parents wanted her to 'settle down' and move to Long Island raise a family and become a housewife (she was married twice and gave birth to a son). Walli once said to me, "Naz do I look like a fucking housewife?

"Her parents would tell her she was an embarrassment to them and her son would be better off if she just didn't come to see him anymore.

"The parents hated her look, the way she dressed...but when she would go for visits she wore velvet nicely fitted pants a black turtleneck sweater, now NYC chic! All black."

Natalie who once ran the "Chocolate Erotica" bakery with her mother says she felt so bad for Walli. "She looked so good and happy when she left, but when she returned she would be pale and exhausted drained from her family basically terrorizing her, that if she didn't change we could make it impossible for you to see your son. There were times she felt it was hopeless and maybe they are right, it would benefit her son if she didn't see him anymore. Then he wouldn't have to see her parents fighting with her in front of him. He wouldn't hear how bad she is, and awful she looks. You can't look like a normal mother. You can't go anywhere without people looking strangely at you. We don't want your son to go through this with you."

Walli really did love her son and I want to make that perfectly clear right here and now.

Such an unfair way of treating a person, I think. Being so utterly judgmental especially to a member of your own family. Indeed, if not a physical one it seems like Walli had to run a mental gauntlet almost every day. It was corporal punishment at its worse with the party being judged guilty forced to run between two rows of soldiers (her parents!) who strike out and attack for petty and selfish reasons.

We could use more of her core values in our world today.

Blessed Be Walli!

MarkBode.com

Vaughn's cartoon interpretation of Walli as depicted in one of his adult comic strips. Obviously, he did appreciate a nice pair of bosoms.

Freddie Prinze.

11.

THE POSSESSION OF FREDDIE PRINZE

CHICO and the *Man* star Freddie Prinze (Sr) had an unusual obsession.

He loved and adored Lenny Bruce to the point where the late standup comedian was literally possessed by him. I mean we're talking about needing the help of an exorcist, whose role Walli had to adapt, at least in this one instance, even though it involved what the White Witch would refer to as a "negative mind set."

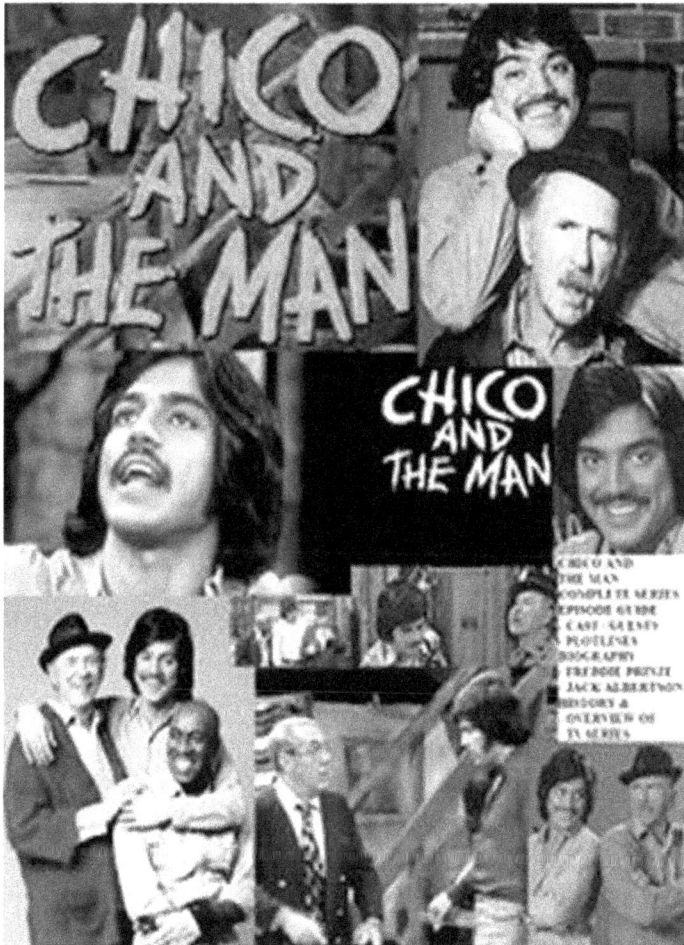

Freddie's show "Chico and the Man" had a huge audience on NBC from 1974 to 1978

Part Hungarian, part Puerto Rican, Prinze was supposed to be taking ballet lessons but ended up performing at "*Catch A Rising Star*" and other dimly lit, smoke filled clubs. His big break came when he appeared on the Johnny Carson Show.

He went over big. He was funny and personable. "The whole world laughs" or so they say. But Freddie was also a troubled and tormented soul.

Freddie was hanging out at Walli's. He was making himself right at home "walking around barefoot," as one scribe puts it, in jest I feel. We don't know for sure the exact status of the relationship between Walli and Freddie or if there was one, there probably wasn't, just a powerful psychic attachment. But Freddie was one of those who had connected himself to Walli, who some might suggest had a strong Svengali-like influence over others seeking much needed psychic advice and spiritual guidance.

He just couldn't take his mind off Lenny Bruce who was best known as a social critic, a satirist who was renowned for his cynical form of comedy which integrated satire, politics, religion, sex and a heavy dose of vulgarity. Bruce had been arrested several times, and even pulled off the stage for his use of four letter words and what was then considered a string of public obscenities.

Was Lenny Bruce a negative influence over Freddie Prinze?

Prinze was so much into Bruce that according to Mark Groubert former "*National Lampoon*" editor, "He took a leaf off of a tree from Lenny's Laurel Canyon house after Lenny's death. Of course, he also dated Kitty Bruce, Lenny's daughter. Kitty used to have the "*Kitty Bruce Band*" in the 80s which I liked."

Lenny drank himself to death and according to numerous sources Prinze was pretty high on drugs most of the time.

Negative spirits who have not moved on to another life often attempt to attach themselves to a person who has similar "negative vibes" about them. Walli could sense such a situation because she was good at reading auras. Anyone, wishing more independent thinking on this subject is invited to read our edition of the book, "*Thirty Years Among The Dead*" by Dr. Carl A. Wickland (February 14, 1861 - November 13, 1945) a licensed psychiatrist and general practitioner.

I guess all of us, who lived during this era, went through this stage. I remember being at Walli's one evening and someone slipped me a Quaalude, a very strong sedative, which I had no experience with. I took it, thinking nothing would happen. A little while later Walli asked me how I liked the downer and I said I didn't think it was having an effect on me. She sort of laughed and said, "Look down." I was eating Chinese takeout and it was all over my lap and the rug. Talk about a bummer. Big in the Sixties and Seventies they were eventually taken off the market. I apologize to whoever had to clean up my Shrimp Chow Fun off the floor. I owe you one.

IN A TRANCE

According to Carol Ann, Walli's long time roomie, Freddie was hearing voices and it was said that Bruce was speaking through him. "Walli played me a tape," Carol says, "where Prinze was in a trance-like state and was possessed by the dark comic. He was cursing like Lenny and really seemed out of it."

Walli tried to help Prinze, but at some point he decided that he was more interested in Elmlark's spell casting to further his own career minded goals and this sort of turned her off and they ended up going their separate ways.

Engaged to Johnny Carson's son at the time, Natalie Kosubal, former owner of Chocolate Erotica whom I met in the early seventies through the band *"Teenage Lust,"* had an inside track on the coming and goings of Prinze. It was Naz who turned me on to Indian food whisking me away from the Academy of Music to a party George Harrison was throwing for Indian sitar player Ravie Shankar. She was a "teenage rock queen" and still is!

"He was more obsessed than possibly possessed. I think he got so high watching and listening and studying Bruce – so much so that he, became Lenny Bruce. He listened to his routines over and over and had studied his mannerisms, so much so that his voice began to sound like Lenny's"

Whatever the connection, Prinze like his mentor ended up extremely depressed, and according to front page headlines, shot himself in the head on January 28, 1977, thus ending a very promising career.

There are those, however, who believe that Freddie's death was NOT a suicide.

"Realist" and counterculture publisher Paul Krassner was telling people that Freddie had been overwhelmed with a variety of conspiracy theories and might have been "targeted." According to Krassner, "They either have to tame you or kill you."

Washington correspondent Mae Brussell says that Freddie was deeply concerned with the Kennedy assassination. In his possession – "in a safe place" the comedian kept a copy of the Zapruder film, which he screened over and over and over, though it had been banned by the FBI for public consumption and was not supposed to be shown or copied under any circumstances. There was a realization that the government was involved in a deep rooted cover-up to keep the facts about the JFK assassination as hush hush as possible.

You, the reader, must ultimately decide what caused Prinze's death. Was it suicide, or was it murder?

Whatever your selection, it still points to the conclusion that Mr. Prinze was a truly troubled soul who had gone to Walli for aid and comfort, and for one reason or another she failed to break through his torment. Prinze's "luck" had run out!

Freddie sought guidance from Walli.

© Helen Hovey Collection.

TAKING WITCHCRAFT SERIOUSLY

Want to take up Witchcraft seriously? Well, there are a number of suggested ways of going about it according to an attractive "White Witch" who resides on the upper east side of Manhattan. Walli Elmlark, a practitioner of white magic, looks the part of a sorceress dressed almost entirely in black and wearing any number of silver crosses and good-luck talismans. Walli recommends a serious attempt be made by all "up-and-coming" witches to learn the Occult sciences, including reading Tarot Cards (an ancient deck of fortune telling cards), Crystal gazing, Palmistry, etc. Also important is a working knowledge of herbs and their uses.

Walli also suggests that all new students of the ancient art of spell-casting spend a good deal of time developing their own psychic abilities. "Many of us have the ability to see the human aura, read palms or receive vibrations about forthcoming situations in our lives and the lives of our friends."

And of course all good witches will need certain "tools" in order to practice. Among the paraphernalia necessary are candles, herbs, incense, oils, etc.

ROCK RAPS OF THE 70's by Timothy Green Beckley and Walli Elmark, Drake Publishers (Illustrated), $3.95; For twenty years we've been told that rock music "is dead." Well, this book proves that the Woodstock nation is alive and well with today's youth. ROCK RAPS is a personal approach to the rock music scene and the people who make it.

It is a journalistic and photographic

ROCK RAPS of the 70's

parade of the well known groups with interviews, anecdotes and experiences of the authors with the groups. All the great names of rock music are here: Jimi Hendrix, Grand Funk Railroad, The Rolling Stones, Jethro Tull, The Jefferson Airplane.

Photographically this book is excellent. More than 65 groups are written about and each are accompanied by action photos taken by such well known rock photographers as Helen Fusco, Lee Marshall and Jeff Meyer. This book is different from all other rock books in that the authors describe in detail the psychic experiences of many of the pop stars. Hendrix was into Voodoo; the Airplane believe that UFOs have landed; Dr. John was raised as a practicioner of white magick in New Orleans, etc.

Timothy Green Beckley is a free lance writer and also director of Global Communications a public relations firm and feature news service. Walli is a speaker on Witchcraft and writes several syndicated columns on rock music. They both live in New York.

Walli and Tim wrote a book "*Rock Raps of the Seventies*" which caused quite a controversy when spoke about the curse on rock stars.

12.

WITH A LITTLE HELP FROM HER FRIENDS

FATHER Time is out to get us all!

As the years roll by many of our friends have exited stage left and are unable to remain with us in the remainder of life's journey.

And people get married, move away, change their name and are lost to us forever.

But there are a few diehards (a perfect word) who remain standing tall among us who will vouch for our sincerity and our role in their lives.

Facebook is a great place to track down those who have "slipped away," but are still out there in the ozone somewhere.

* * * * * * * *

NATALI KOSUBAL ("NAZ) - OWNER OF CHOCOLATE EROTICA AND CONFIDENT OF WALLI'S

Walli and I met in the lobby of the Academy of Music during one of the shows. I was with the band *"Teenage Lust."* We were both wearing some very interesting vintage-antique jewelry, and were both admiring and complimenting each other on our choice of pieces we had on that night. So we began chatting about the jewelry that attracted us, if there was a meaning behind each piece, a "psychic" connection to each piece we wore.

It's like when you meet someone for the very first time it's a feeling you have, like you have known them forever. Its innocent, honest, you clearly understand each other, feeling close, having this instant connection.

Whenever Walli and I went to an event, we would walk around, talk and smile. She'd turn to me and say, "Look over there, you see so and so, what colors of auras do you see?" Walli always wanted me to use my harnessed power, to open myself to what is around. Walli also practiced telepathy. Lol, funny my mother always knew where I was or what I was doing without telling her. We had a very strong relationship and connection. Walli must have picked up on that.

Yes, well, when friends are in tune to each other's senses, it seems they can read each other's thoughts.

Walli was definitely one of the most interesting individuals I have met in my life.

Natali - Naz - Kosubal was a close confident of Walli's.

* * * * * * * *

JOHN MINETOLA - HEAD USHER ACADEMY OF MUSIC

My situation then: I now live in Dearfield Beach, Florida. At the time I knew Walli, I was studying Cinema History at NYU, working at the Fillmore East and then at the Academy of Music after the Fillmore closed. As an usher and security guy, I met a lot of rockers (sat with John Lennon and Frank Zappa after they played together, for instance) and dealt with a lot of fans, too. I did some handyman major remodeling of promoter Howard Stein's office and knew his staff well.

Caption: Head usher Academy of Music - John Minetola.

Just before meeting Walli, I worked a "*Who*" concert at Forest Hills in Queens. One of the other security guys was stabbed to death by a fan in the line to get in. Another security guy was hospitalized. "*The Who*" invited us all to a party that night. Keith Moon cut his hand from smashing a glass. I spoke with Leslie West of Mountain. Stephen Stills passed out drunk and some gorgeous blonds dragged him out to his limo. I got a guitar neck that Pete Townshend had smashed, but gave it away to somebody I knew. I didn't see the value at the time, since many nights were like this.

Fall of '71, outside of work, I did meet and go out with Penny Ashton ("*Vogue*" magazine cover model,) Faith Langford (model and actress,) Dick Shawn (actor in "*The Producers*") and a few rockers. Things were very busy for me and as fun as anybody says those times were in NYC.

However, I did keep a journal, and it backs up my memories of Walli.

December 13, 1971. I had chatted with Walli before and let her into the Academy a few times. Knew she was a writer for "*Circus*." This night was a "*Mountain*" concert, and Walli was hanging around in the back of the concert hall. We exchanged phone numbers, and I remember that she was fun and intriguing to talk to. She looked just like that picture with the green streak in her hair, the rhinestone teardrop on her cheek. I often wore bright green Beatle-boot type shoes and we talked about how the hair streak and my shoes matched.

December 27, around midnight, I went uptown to Walli's apartment and we talked until just before dawn. Mostly about how difficult her life was. She said she knew I was a good witch. We did communicate even when we weren't together. She said she could light a candle, concentrate on me, and I would call her to ask what she wanted me for. She gave me a silver ring, which I still have, and I think it gave some amount of control over me.

On New Year's Eve, we were out for a bite, and the waiter said he liked our costumes, although we were just dressed as always.

Walli had a few girls who would come over to practice Wicca around the pentagram on the living room floor. I think one of them went on the road with a roadie for the "Grateful Dead" in the summer of '72. I remember being a good listener to those girls and their stories of problems at home, etc. Walli's torn soul needed more attention though, and I tried to make her feel some comfort. She was very giving of her strength to many people around her and yet she needed to keep her demons away, too. Walli wasn't doing drugs or alcohol in excess (although the stories of the times would make it seem like everybody was.) She did have a lot of guilt laid on her by her parents about her rock'n'roll, witchcraft lifestyle, but her spells did help with getting that out of her head.

Walli got passes to concerts, limousines, albums and some great treats from "Circus" magazine. We took a limo to see Al Green (and others) at the Apollo in Harlem. We were the only white people in the audience. Al Green was just breaking out, released "Let's Stay Together" in January 1972. His live act was a lot like James Brown had done, shown in the TAMI Show movie. Walli took me to see Bill Withers in a small club in Greenwich Village. One of the most sincere performers I had ever seen (and I saw a lot of music!!) I don't know if Walli wrote about it for "Circus." As much as we talked, we didn't talk about her writing. (I write professionally now, did a monthly article about boats for 25 years until recently, etc.) Funny that Walli and I laughed and talked about friends, music and maybe some deep stuff about Magick. She did understand performers and their personalities in a time when shows were less rehearsed. The person showed through in those days. Walli did look for goodness in the song lyrics, too.

We never broke up but Walli was getting busy with Robert Fripp in late spring of 1972, and I did a cross-country motorcycle ride, and then spent the rest of the summer on Cape Cod.

BIOGRAPHICALLY SPEAKING

Walli's audition photo for her brief off Broadway acting career. Said to have been used to gain employment at the Playboy Club (as coat check gal).

Walli told me she was born in 1938, although ancestry.com says 1939.

I think she was doing some acting in the mid-1950s, and the head shot says she was in Boston Summer Theater in 1959.

I'm sure you've seen the internet posts that say she was a Playboy club bunny in 1960's.

Her dad was Harry Eugene Elmlark, very conservative newsman and of the "*Washington Star.*" Very conservative. They even syndicated William F. Buckley's column. He passed away in 1980.

Walli's mom, Lillian, had Walli's son with her sometimes while I was seeing Walli. They spoke often on the phone, and Walli did miss him a lot. Lillian did not approve of Walli, and did chastise her on the phone. I think Walli's son, Kevin, was with his father most of the time, but I never heard Walli talk to or about her ex-husband.

Walli lived at 310 E 65th Street. Apt 2-E. She lit a BBQ charcoal grill just inside the window, hoping the smoke would blow out the open window. Firemen put it out.

She was writing for "*Circus*" when I met her in the fall of 1971. I didn't see her again after the summer of 1972. I guess Sandy Becker moved in with her for a couple years starting in 1972

The Bowie pool exorcism was in 1975, I think from your posts.

I don't know if she passed away in 1976, according to ancestry.com, or 3-4 years later according to Sandy Becker. (Either 1980 or 81 - TGB)

Walli was certainly an important influence on me.

* * * * * * * *

CAROL LINDA GONZALEZ - STUDENT NY OCCULT CENTER

Carol Linda Gonzalez met Walli at the Occult Center. Recently, she spoke at the NYC Tolkien Festival.

Walli was part of Tim Beckley's metaphysical center, where you could hear talks and attend workshops on UFOs and paranormal topics. I was mostly attracted to Tim and his UFO accounts. Walli was an exciting surprise! I attended talks held at her home, an interesting place that had a magic circle on the floor at its entrance. And yes, I was already interested in spiritual matters and the occult before meeting her.

Walli was the first working witch I ever met. She was my teenaged idea of an enchantress. She was beautiful, magical and was part of a world I didn't know. I never met anyone like her before.

To be honest, I can't say I was specifically attracted to her teachings at the time I met her. I didn't know much about modern witchcraft at the time. Walli looked like the kind of woman I wanted to be. So, I listened. My purpose in attending Tim's talks was to engage in discussion with others who shared similar interests. Walli was the unexpected benefit. I knew absolutely nothing about her. Her connection to the music world and her work with glamorous personalities was unknown to me at the time.

She never did any spells for me. What I learned from her was the ritual structure that is the basics of magick as practiced today. It was the start of my personal practice. I made sure to ask questions which she answered. I remember she wrote a little book that I enjoyed. Sadly, I lost it through the years. What I remember best was her elaborate signature. Maybe she worked on it as a magical sigil.

At the time I met Walli, I had a beginner's interest in the occult, Wicca, and other forms of spiritual practices, but no experience. Walli was the first working witch I had ever met. My exchanges with her were all about the workings of magick. I'd love to see her magick circle again. I wonder if anyone has a picture of it. Today, I'd probably understand it better.

When I reconnected with Tim on Facebook, Walli was one of the first people I asked about. That's when I first heard about her passing. It saddened me. As I recall, she was undergoing an emotional upheaval over her separation and the custody of a child. She said it was so overwhelming to her that she accidentally injured herself with a knife once.

Overall, Walli influenced the spiritual methods I used to help me overcome personal challenges that came my way in ensuing years. That's why I will always remember her!

* * * * * * * *

KEN CURRIER - MY LIFE WITH WALLI

Note by Tim Beckley – I have known Ken for centuries it seems. I first was introduced to him by Walli. Later, when Ken married Sue, a beautiful Australian model, the couple did it with a bit of fanfare tying the knot on top of the Empire State Building. Acting as an impromptu publicist we got their wedding vows on the front page of the "*Daily News*" (circulation about 3 million at the time – when people still knew what newsstands were meant for).

After ten years in television production, in 1981 Ken and Sue founded a software company making games for early home computers. After selling the company to a firm in Miami, the couple founded another game company which they took public in 1995 and sold to Activison Bizzard. After the sale, they founded another game company and then declared that three start-ups were enough. Today they are consultants for a conversational artificial intelligence software start up and travel as much as possible. Ken is currently working on a novel. We had some good times together back in the Seventies and promoted the First (and last!) International Glitter Ball at the Hotel Diplomat in Time Square and spent weekends at Edgar Winters estate in Long Island, while the band was on tour (with permission I should state).

Ken Currier circa early Seventies.　　Mr. Currier now.

ENTERING THE WITCHES CIRCLE

There I was, just a dumb-assed kid, barely twenty, from a sleepy little suburban town near Boston. I was working for a Speakers Bureau in the television department, basically as a schlep. It was late in the afternoon, and I was rushing to finish my work so I could take off and meet my girlfriend for dinner.

And then my life changed!

I heard a commotion in the conference room, a cluster of booking agents, all male, were piling out of the room, looking happy and joking frantically. The White Witch of New York came in to meet all the agents and we hooked up to possibly get some bookings as a speaker at colleges.

This is when I first met Walli.

I wandered closer to get a better look. She was thin, elegant with long dark hair, nearly covering her face. It was hard to catch a glimpse beneath her thick long mane, but I could see that she was beautiful in a dark and moody way. She wasn't tall but her heels gave her a few extra inches. She didn't walk, she floated and her layers of dress and scarves flowed behind her.

We locked eyes and she headed straight for me. Honestly, I was kind of scared, being just a dumb-assed kid, but she introduced herself and put me at ease. The wisecracking agents stood back and stared. What the hell did this beautiful creature see in him, they joked. My status rose rapidly.

Three weeks later, I said goodbye to my ex-girlfriend (or good riddance as she would characterize it), dumped the lease on my roach infested Cambridge tenement and packed my meager belongings into a cheap rental car, while Walli waited patiently in the passenger seat.

And five hours later we saw the bright lights of Manhattan, as we crested the Triborough Bridge and rolled onto Harlem River Drive. Twenty minutes after that staggering scene, we pulled up to a swanky high rise apartment building on the Upper East Side and unloaded my possessions into my new home.

When she opened the door, there was a huge pentagram painted on the floor of the entryway. I knew something was up.

That's how it started, quickly, before I even had a chance to think this through. It was like a spell was cast upon me. And of course, as I eventually figured out, that's exactly what happened. If you think that this stuff is hogwash, I can tell you that she was powerful.

In her quiet, introspective way she would somehow make things better for people she loved, people she cared about. I have no idea how; I was just, as she referred to me, a mortal, living on earth, not in a spiritual plane.

She took me all over New York, mostly in the dark of night, to meet strange and mysterious people; to secret occult bookstores and stores that sold the accouterments of the Wicca religion, the religion the good witches, the white witches practiced.

We'd go to covens and events that cast group spells to drive away the influences of the bad witches. The speaker's bureau booked Walli all over the country. I joined her tour briefly and it was fun but there was some smoke and mirrors. Lots of "bad witches" were turning up at her appearances to try to out spell her.

Walli was mainly a very strong spiritual healer. People she cared about seemed to thrive. They often became more assertive, as if the Wicca religion worked as a form of feminism and female empowerment. Did it have anything to do with the many spells she cast, the positive beliefs she enriched people with?

I can cite one case that, to this day, astonished me. It was so surreal that I'm not even sure it happened. But I'm pretty sure it did.

We were at an occult convention, lots of witches, both good and bad, spitting vibes at one another. Plus warlocks, elves, nymphs, and other uncategorized believers.

A lovely young girl cautiously maneuvered her way through the crowded aisles and walked up to Walli and touched her cheek. I could see this beautiful young girl was blind. She was feeling Walli's face to get to know her. Walli seemed to understand this girl's desires. They spent the rest of the day in deep conversation.

Weeks went by, maybe even months. I was just working hard at a new television production company job and spending my nights with Walli, wandering the city's magical and exotic underbelly.

One cloudy winter Sunday, Walli and I were spending a quiet afternoon, out of the cold, in her comfortable living room when the doorman announced a visitor. A few minutes later there was a faint knock and the front door slowly creaked open. There she was – the lovely blind girl – walking confidently through the foyer and into the living room where she and Walli embraced for a long time.

She looked at me and smiled. She was no longer blind.

* * * * * * *

What a wonderful, fitting conclusion.

Walli if you're "out there" or "back here" by now thanks for everything and by all means BLESSED BE!

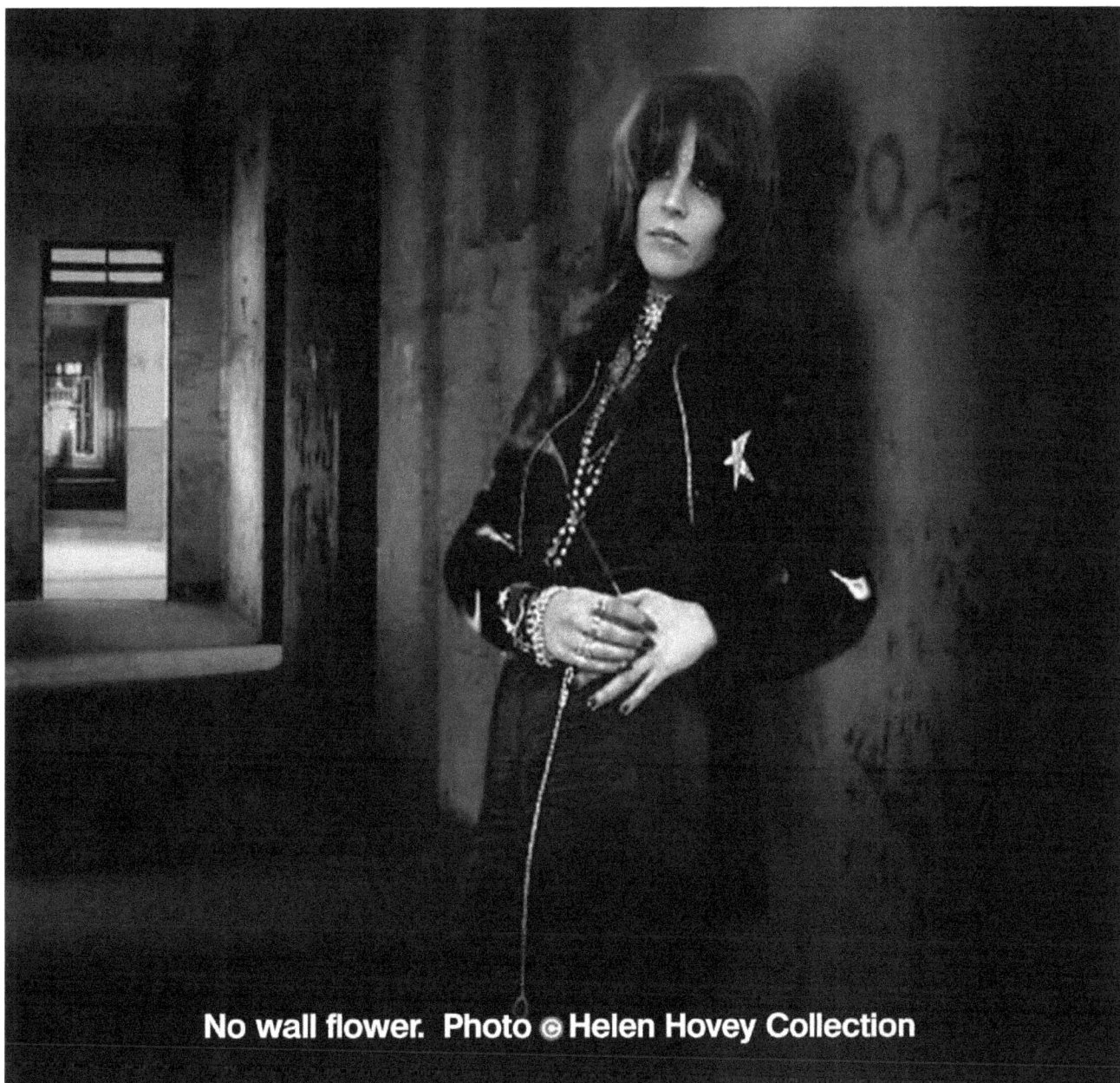

No wall flower. Photo © Helen Hovey Collection

www.ingramcontent.com/pod-product-compliance
Lightning Source LLC
Chambersburg PA
CBHW062104090426
42741CB00015B/3332